Tips and Traps for
Getting Started as a
REAL ESTATE
AGENT

ROBERT IRWIN

AMERICA'S #1 REAL ESTATE EXPERT

Tips and Traps for Getting Started as a

REAL ESTATE AGENT

McGraw-Hill

New York   Chicago   San Francisco   Lisbon   London
Madrid   Mexico City   Milan   New Delhi   San Juan
Seoul   Singapore   Sydney   Toronto

The *McGraw-Hill* Companies

4 5 6 7 8 9 0   DOC/DOC   0 9 8

ISBN=13: 978-0-07-146336-2
ISBN=10: 0-07-146336-4

Realtor® is a registered collective membership mark that identifies a real estate professional who is a member of the NATIONAL ASSOCIATION OF REALTORS® and abides by its strict Code of Ethics.

This publication is designed to provide accurate and authoritative information in regard to the subject matter covered. It is sold with the understanding that neither the author nor the publisher is engaged in rendering legal, accounting, or other professional service. If legal advice or other expert assistance is required, the services of a competent professional person should be sought.
> —*From a Declaration of Principles jointly adopted by a Committee of the American Bar Association and a Committee of Publishers*

McGraw-Hill books are available at special quantity discounts to use as premiums and sales promotions, or for use in corporate training programs. For more information, please write to the Director of Special Sales, McGraw-Hill Professional, Two Penn Plaza, New York, NY 10121-2298. Or contact your local bookstore.

Library of Congress Cataloging-in-Publication Data
Irwin, Robert
    Tips and traps for getting started as a real estate agent / by Robert Irwin.
    p.   cm.
    Includes index.
    ISBN 0-07-146336-4 (alk. paper)
    1. Real estate business. 2. Real estate agents. I. Title.

HD1379.I666 2006
333.33068'1—dc22   2006005493

Contents

Preface

This book is for agents, by an agent. Those just getting started will benefit most, although experienced agents should find many of the tips particularly helpful.

I've written many successful books on real estate, aimed at investors and consumers. Given that history, I felt a bit of trepidation taking on a project aimed exclusively at agents. My fears were unwarranted. After all, I've had a real estate broker's license for 43 continuous years, as of this writing. (I was one of the youngest people to get a broker's license in California, at just 21 years old.)

As soon as I sat down at my computer, the words began flowing out. It was as if I had waited my whole life to write this book. I discovered I had so many stories to tell, suggestions to make, and lessons to offer that I could barely type fast enough to get it all down. Of course, giving credit where due, a lot of the material comes from other agents and brokers with whom I've worked and from whom I've learned.

But, let's be realistic. No book is going to turn you into an instant success at selling real estate. In fact, no speaker, guru, or mentor can do that. Only you can do that for yourself.

However, this book can show you exciting and fulfilling ways to get off to a quick and positive start.

If you're just beginning your career in real estate, the horizon is open to you, the opportunities unlimited. However, the pitfalls along the way are many and deep. We all know that too many agents who begin never actually succeed.

That, however, doesn't have to be you. You can become the *super-agent,* who makes hundreds of thousands of dollars, sometimes millions in commissions.

The first year, the first month, indeed even the first week are critical. How you get started is the best predictor of how you'll end up.

So, leap right in. Begin turning the pages to learn about making big commissions and developing a lifelong rewarding career.

Robert Irwin
www.robertirwin.com

Acknowledgments

The author wants to thank the many real estate professionals who helped in providing information, stories, and advice in the preparation of this book. Also, a special thanks to Jason Wolenik who runs *www.robertirwin.com* and who provided insight, research, and backup writing.

Introduction:
What's Involved in
Being an Agent?

There are well over a million real estate agents nationwide as of this writing. If you're already one of them, then proceed immediately to Chapter 1 to learn how to get started being hugely successful. If, on the other hand, you're just considering joining their ranks, here's how you become an agent.

In all 50 states in order to represent a seller or a buyer in the sale, or leasing, of real estate you must be licensed. This usually involves two things. The first is getting a real estate broker (someone who is fully licensed) to sponsor you as a salesperson (someone who works under the tutelage of a broker). The second is completing specified course work on real estate, the third is passing a state exam.

Note

In some states if you have a college degree in a related field, such as business, you may not need to take the course work.

Of course, you must also normally prove to the state that you're not a felon and are a person of good character.

The real estate salesperson course work is not usually extensive and the test isn't usually considered to be very difficult. Many people pass it after taking a short course. Others pass after simply reading up on the field from a book. Courses and books designed to help you pass your state's course work and exam are plentiful. Check the Internet and your local bookstore. I find the *Anthony* books and courses to be particularly thorough.

Once you pass your salesperson test, you'll normally be required to serve an apprenticeship under a broker, typically for two years. After that, if there have been no complaints against you, you'll be allowed to sit for your own broker's license, which involves passing a more rigorous test.

Be sure you understand the terminology of the field, as it can be confusing:

Agent. A person licensed to sell (or lease) real estate for others.

Broker. A licensed person who can work for himself or herself and collect commissions.

Salesperson. A licensed person who must work under the auspices of a broker.

Realtor.® A broker member of the National Association of Realtors (NAR), a trade organization .

Realtor Associate. A salesperson member of the NAR.

Ready to get started on a highly rewarding career?!

Begin by contacting a broker who will be willing to sponsor you. Many brokers advertise that they are looking for new salespeople. (See also Chapter 3, on choosing the right broker.) Your broker will help you register with your state's department of real estate, so you can get underway and take your exam.

1

The Realities of Realty

A *super-agent* can make over a million dollars a year in commissions. Unfortunately, the vast majority of agents are not *super* but only *average*. An *average* agent can only expect to make around $38,000 a year (U.S. Census Bureau).

Do you want to be a *super-agent* or *just average?*

The *average* agent will typically work over 40 hours a week, only take a few days off each year, and still has the burden of the usual expenses—car, business clothing, medical insurance, and so on. In truth these agents may be barely hanging on by their fingernails, particularly if they have a family to support. The *average* agent may be making a living, but is certainly not living well. For comparison, an *average* Postal worker makes about $46,000 annually. (This is not to say anything against Post Office employees—at one point in my career I enjoyed being one!)

On the other hand, an *above-average* agent makes up to $90,000 a year. This agent puts in as much as 60 hours a week and may sell as many as 20 to 30 or more homes a year. About 1 in 5 agents fall into this second category.

Being *above-average* certainly pays better, but at the cost of hustling to close roughly two or three deals a month. This agent is probably running ragged trying to keep up.

TIP

As those in the business know, the word "agent" can mean either broker or salesperson. A broker is one who can collect a commission, list property, and carry out all the normal duties involved in real estate sales. A salesperson can only work under the auspices of a broker. Getting stated normally means working as a salesperson.

And then there's the *super-agent.* He or she makes between $90,000 and $1 million or more a year. And this person sells about around 15 to 30 properties during that time. This agent puts in around 40 hours a week, depending on how income flows in. Many expenses are covered by someone else. We're now talking the top 5 percent. Out of every 100 agents, only 5 or less, fit into this category. (It's a great place to be!)

Notice any discrepancies?

The *super-agent* isn't spending more time or selling more properties. Yet, this agent's income is substantially higher than that of other agents. How can this be?

Don't Let the Numbers Game Fool You

Today the average property sells for around $225,000. Assuming a 6 percent commission (national statistics suggest that the true average commission is actually closer to 5 percent) split 50-50 between brokers, then 50-50 between broker and salesperson, the *average* salesperson takes home about $3,375 per average deal. It's easy to see that it takes a lot of these deals to make $50,000 a year.

TIP

The better the agent, the better the split. Top agents get as much as 70-30 or even 80-20 splits (the big number, of course, going to the salesperson, the smaller number to the broker).

As any agent in the business will tell you, however, making about a dozen deals a year is pretty darn good. Now, consider this. The agent making a million dollars a year, based on these same figures, would have to close 296 deals a year. That's over three closings every four days!

Yes, there might be an agent or two nationwide who actually does this—but darn few. For the rest of us, it's a wholly unrealistic number. Don't believe those gurus who tell you the *only* way to increase your income is by increasing your sales volume. It's a fool's gambit—and the surest way to go out of business.

TRAP

 Most economies of scale do *not* apply to real estate. In a factory the cost per widget for 1,000 might be half the cost per unit of making just 10 widgets. But, real estate is a service industry. What closes deals and brings you referrals is personal service. And you have to maintain a high level of service, whether you're closing a dozen or a 100 deals a year. The more deals you try to close, the *harder*, not *easier*, it is to maintain that good service.

How Do They Do It?

Yet there are still those real estate agents who do make between $90,000 and $1 million or more a year. How do they accomplish this?

The answer is an old adage, they don't work harder, they work smarter. *Super-agents* make more money because they do three important things:

- They sell more *expensive* properties.
- They get *bigger percentages* of commissions on *bigger* deals.
- They *invest in real estate* themselves, and a significant portion of their income (and referrals) come from their owned properties.

In this book we're going to see how you can become a *super-agent,* one who isn't killing himself or herself trying to fulfill unrealistic quotas. We're going to look at techniques that boost your income. We're going to see how to make big money as a real estate agent by developing a life-long career from which you can retire early. (You *do* want to retire early, don't you?)

In short, this book is based in the reality of the real estate business as it is. We're here concerned with what works, not with what plays well to an audience.

TRAP

I once knew an extremely popular real estate speaker who was constantly looking for "zingers." These were quick phrases and witticisms that sounded good and inspired audiences. When I asked him if they really worked, he replied, "Who cares?" Of course, many speakers do provide excellent insights and information. It's a matter of separating the wheat from the chaff.

What Kind of a Career Do You Want?

There are at least four popular tracks for the active real estate agent today (not including becoming an appraiser, mortgage broker, escrow officer, and so on). They are:

- The solitary lister-seller
- The team player
- The company builder
- The modern "traditionalist"

All have merits, as we'll see. However, first let's consider something old fashioned, the traditional agent.

The Traditional Real Estate Career

Today, it's popular to pooh-pooh the old, traditional agent. This is a person who was a generalist. He or she sold houses and strip malls and farms and anything else that came in over the transom.

"Old fashioned," "outdated," and "can't keep up" are expressions I've heard used to describe this person.

Yet, as is so often the case, those who are eager to be modern, to be on the leading edge (sometimes called the "bleeding edge" in the high-tech business) often end up throwing out the baby with the bathwater. There are certain essential features of the traditional real estate agent that are well worth preserving and, if followed, can turn today's novice into a *super-agent.*

The Old-Fashioned Way

Leo (his real name) was an immigrant. He came here from the "old" country (Yugoslavia, actually), got his citizenship, and wanted to make money in order to have a better life (a universal ambition for most immigrants, as well as for the rest of us). So in the 1950s he studied hard for his real estate exam and, after failing to pass the test several times, finally got his salesman's license. (The failures were because of his difficulty with the language, not because of any lack of intelligence on his part.)

I remember him telling me how surprised he was that once he got his license, the money didn't start rolling in. "I only began learning real estate *after* they licensed me."

He signed up with the largest office in town at that time (this was long before franchises), and quickly found an experienced agent who agreed to "show him the business." Leo went out on listing presentations with his agent-friend and quickly got the hang of it. Soon he was out there on his own and bringing in more listings than others in his office. It turned out his difficulty with the English language was a plus, because other immigrants with similar problems felt comfortable dealing with him.

During his second year as a salesperson, he worked with several other agents on a "big deal" involving a commercial center selling for hundreds of thousands of dollars (a lot of money for those days). Later that same year he got into farms selling several big plots of land.

As the second year of his apprenticeship neared its end, he studied hard to get his broker's license. After several failed attempts, he finally succeeded. He became a real estate broker. He opened an office and struck out on his own.

During the next 30 years, Leo had good times and bad. He was known for being straightforward and extremely honest. Once, he even returned a commission to a client who was unhappy with the way the deal went. (That's something almost unheard of today!)

Over time, his reputation spread, and he established a large clientele that came to him when they wanted to buy or sell. He achieved the Holy Grail of real estate agents, an almost totally referral-based business. Sellers sought him out, he didn't need to go looking for listings. And ready-to-go buyers kept walking in the front door of his office.

During this time many good deals appeared, and when he had the funds he bought property on his own. When he didn't have the cash, he bought with partners. He owned homes, bare land, apartment buildings, strip malls, and more. Yet, he spent less and less time in the business, concentrating on the bigger deals. He started a property management firm to handle his properties, as well as those of his clients, and he "hired" several salespeople who lived mainly off the smaller home listings he produced. If he were in a law firm, he'd be called a "rainmaker." He brought in business.

Needless to say, Leo retired well. He was respected in his community. People consulted him, even in retirement, when they had a real estate problem. And he wasn't short of money.

Leo's was the traditional real estate career. He was an independent broker who ran his own office. He was a generalist who handled any kind of real property deals. Most important to him, he had time for a life outside his career.

It should be obvious that there's a great deal to be said for the traditionalist in real estate. Of course, as anyone in the business today will tell you, with the frenetic competition, with the Internet, with franchises, with savvy sellers and buyers, it's hard to imagine anyone surviving as a traditionalist. Today an independent and a generalist, except in some small-town situations, has a very small chance of success.

Nevertheless, there are three important techniques that Leo used that we need to remember:

- He worked toward selling *more expensive* properties.
- Because he was his own broker, he got *bigger percentages* of commissions on *bigger* deals
- He always invested in real estate.

That was then, this is now. Real estate is a different kind of animal today.

The Solitary Lister-Seller

Today probably the most popular track in real estate for the beginner is the home lister-seller. This agent spends most of his or her time finding home listings and trying to develop buyer referrals from them. The hope is for the "double pop" or "double bubble"—getting a buyer for their listed property so the agent represents both sides of the deal and gets a whole commission (no splits). Sometimes it happens. Most of the time, it doesn't.

Of course, the emphasis is on listing. You don't have to be in the business long before the expression, "Those who list, last," is ground into you. Any number of brokers, mentors, and books will tell you (as if they've just discovered it themselves) that the key to being a successful agent is to get listings. The more listings you have, not only the more sellers you'll have, but the more buyers you'll develop from those listings, and the result will be more total sales.

TIP

It's not simply leads. It's getting solid leads that you can convert into listings.

Thus, today some agents try to become what I call "listing machines."

The trouble is that most agents who are simply out to list and sell homes end up as *average*. No matter how much time they devote or enthusiasm they have, they don't get ahead. They are on a volume-only treadmill. As soon as their volume slips, there goes their income. Their life is frenetic, constantly looking for the new lead, seldom getting that solid referral.

The Team Player

Yet another career track has become popular recently—the agent as team player. Working under the theory that two minds (or three or more) are better than one, agents band to together to form teams. They share listings, clients, and commissions. This is most frequently found as husband-and-wife teams. However, any two or more people can become team players.

A few teams, particularly husbands and wives working together, have had spectacular results in different parts of the country. Several have become top producers, million-dollar agents.

On the other hand, team playing is fraught with peril. If there aren't enough sales, as can happen, then too few commissions end up getting split between the team. That leads to hard feelings about who is doing the most work and who deserves the bigger slice of the dwindling pie. Few teams last a long time.

Company Building

Finally, there's the track where an agent wants to "grow the business." He or she typically starts out independently, then gets a broker's license and becomes an office manager in a franchise, and eventually opens his or her own office.

The trouble is that the skills required to build a company (hire the right people; manage money, time, and staff; raise capital, and so on) are not the same skills required to be a great salesperson. Thus, it is often the case that the person who succeeds in sales fails at company building.

Building a company, and a real estate empire, is the goal of many aspiring new agents. However, before you jump onto this track, it's important to know what you really want. While it can be the road to riches, not everyone, perhaps not even most people, want or are suited to the administrative and managerial type of career.

TRAP

 Remember the old proverb—be careful what you wish for, you may get it!

The Modern "Traditionalist"

This is an agent who is open to *all* possibilities. He or she will list and will work with buyers. This agent spends the early months and years of a real estate career discovering and then refining his or her strengths—exploring *all* avenues of real estate.

Of course, what we're talking about is a budding *super-agent.* Sometimes this person will discover a niche where he or she excels, whether it be residential, commercial, appraisal, mortgage banking, or some other area of real estate. This person could, of course, narrowly become the world's greatest lister, or make a fortune within a team, or open a whole new franchise company. But, the budding super-agent doesn't limit herself or himself to just those possibilities. She or he may do all of them! Or something else.

We'll spend the rest of this book talking about this *super-agent.*

Which Track Will You Take?

As you're getting started, each of these four tracks (and possibly others) are open to you. The choice you make is vitally important. Pick the wrong track and you could quickly wash out. Pick the right one, and wealth, an early retirement, and lots of fun will be yours. Always remember that as a real estate agent the possibilities available to you are endless.

There is perhaps no other occupation in this country with such a low cost of entrance (typically around $100 for a license plus whatever you pay for course work to get it) yet with such a high opportunity for success. You can indeed make millions in real estate. As we've seen, about 5 percent in the field are *super-agents.*

Just as there are no limitations, however, there are also no guarantees. In real estate you have ultimate freedom—you can go high, or you can flop. Your future is almost entirely in your own hands. Through career choices, self-motivation, careful observation, and hard work, you can become just what you want to be.

2

Seven Simple Truths About Getting Started

Back in the 1950s, my father retired as a successful grocer with a nest egg that he thought would carry him through his later life. It only took a few years, however, and the inflation of the time to convince him that he needed to go back to work.

Being a grocer was no longer an option; it was physically too strenuous. So he looked around and eventually decided on real estate. That began a 30-year successful second career for him.

I suspect that most people who go into real estate make the choice in a similar fashion. They hunt around for something that will meet their needs and sooner or later stumble upon selling property. I've heard kids say they wanted to be a fireman, or a cop, or a doctor, a lawyer, or even a CEO. But never have I heard of a kid who dreamt of being a Realtor. It's something that you sort of drift into.

There are reasons for this, and we are going to look at some of them below. But what's important when you're starting out is that you do so with a big dash of reality. If you're getting into this business, there are at least seven truths that, while simple, are immutable. Put them under the heading of "things people forgot to tell me."

The following are the seven.

Truth 1: The Entry Costs Are Amazingly Low

You want to be a doctor? You've got undergraduate school, medical school, residency, and then possibly advanced training ahead of you. What's the cost for all those years? Today, it could be anywhere from $250,000 to $400,000, depending on the quality of the schools. It can be less than that if you want to be a lawyer, but it's still a pretty penny. Want to be a commercial pilot? Even if you've gotten your basic training in the military, there's still getting rated on a commercial plane, and that could cost tens of thousands of dollars. Teachers normally need a four-year college degree and an additional year of teacher education, perhaps $50,000 at a state-sponsored school. Even a cosmetologist must go to school for months, if not for a year or longer.

But not a real estate agent.

As you should know, to become a real estate salesperson, all that you need is for a broker to sponsor you and then pass an exam. At minimum, you can buy a couple of books, study up, pass the exam, and then you're licensed to go. In many states the total cost can be as little as $100. If you need a course to help you pass the exam, then add in around $350 more.

One of the biggest inducements to getting started in real estate is that, when compared to other professions, the entry costs are without doubt the lowest. Perhaps that's something that you've thought about yourself when you decided to go for it.

Truth 2: There Usually Are No Formal Education Requirements

Want to get started selling real estate? Most states have three basic requirements to be a salesperson:

1. You must be at least 18 years of age.

2. You must be of good character.

3. You must pass an exam.

The financial and educational requirements for the other professions looked at previously are formidable. It's typically a long haul to get in these other careers.

But not real estate. In many states you're not even required to have finished high school. You simply must be able to read, write, and think well enough to pass the licensing exam.

In a sense, real estate is a totally equal-opportunity profession. Almost anyone who has the desire to get in can do so. (Of course, if you've been convicted of a felony or serious misdemeanor, the door may be closed to you.)

That's why there is an unusually large number of immigrants in real estate. People who have come to the United States from foreign countries seeking to make their fortune naturally migrate to the field. Often they do exceptionally well, particularly when selling to those who speak their native tongue.

That's also why there are a large number of young people who either don't want to go to college, have dropped out, or have graduated from college but haven't really made a career choice. The field makes for a great opportunity to do something "outside the box."

And it also explains why there are so many retirees from other professions (teachers, military, public employees, and so on) in the field. They don't need to spend years going to school to move in and move on.

Truth 3: The Amount You Can Make Is Unlimited

Most professions have earning ceilings. A teacher, for example, who works at it for 20 years may max out at around $50,000. A welder (who spent years getting licensed) may make $80,000 at the top. Even a medical general practitioner may rarely be able to make over $250,000.

But what's the maximum that a *super-agent* can make?

Today there are a few agents who are approaching $100 million in sales. That translates into multimillions of dollars in income for them. And their numbers are increasing every year.

Those who are members of million-dollar clubs have increased dramatically along with the values in real estate.

In short, there is no ceiling on what you can make in real estate. And that's part of what makes it such an attractive profession. Where else can you get in for a few hundred dollars, with almost no educational qualifications, and yet have the potential to make millions?

Truth 4: It May Be Three Months or Longer Before You Get Your First Commission Check

While the previous three "truths" are probably understood by most who get into the field, for some reason this one seems to slip by. I suspect everyone knows it down deep. But, each person figures that it will be different for him or her.

The problem really arises because most people getting started in real estate have an employee mentality. If you've worked for an employer all your life, then you've been conditioned to getting that paycheck every week or two. In fact, chances are you've been living hand to mouth for that paycheck.

Selling real estate, however, is a totally different kind of animal. Here there are no paychecks. (Some call a commission a "paycheck," but in reality that's a misnomer and falls back on the old concept of employee/employer.)

For some, this concept is almost too hard to conceive. You may spend 60 or more hours a week in your first year selling property, and yet the person for whom you work doesn't pay you anything. (Some brokers will allow a "draw" against future earnings, but usually only for experienced agents.) This goes against everything that's common sense in the relationships between employers and employees.

TRAP

 Usually you are considered an "independent contractor." What that essentially means is that although the broker may provide office space, phone, advertising, and other aids, you basically work for yourself. You're the equivalent of an entrepreneur. You're self-employed.

For those of us who have been self-employed most of our adult lives, making the transition to real estate sales isn't really that hard. If you were selling widgets before, chances are now you can sell property. On the other hand, for some the real reason for failure is never getting past this stumbling block. Until you can get over the employer/employee mentality, you'll never succeed in real estate. In this field, you're your own boss. While your broker may have certain "assignments" for you, it's basically up to you to decide what to do and when to do it.

What all of this means is that until you've sold a property and collected a commission, you won't get paid. You could easily go without income for three months or far longer.

Consider: On the day you get your license, you list your mother's house. (She's been waiting patiently for you to get started before putting the family home up for sale; that's what mothers do.) It takes a month to find a buyer. It takes another month to close escrow. And then it takes a while longer before your share of the commission finally gets to you.

Therefore, under the *best* of circumstances, it's likely to be a couple of months before your first check arrives. And then what do you do for an encore? Most of us only have one mother. How long before the next sale and commission?

You get the idea. Getting started can be a long and drawn-out process. In the first year I sold real estate, adjusted for today's dollars, I made less than $25,000. That's probably high for many beginning agents. (Of course, later years were significantly better!)

All of which means that you're going to need a big nest egg. You need to have six months or more saved up for expenses. Or your spouse needs to bring in enough to keep you going. Or you need to be amazingly thrifty. Or ...?

TRAP

The first few months are critical. During that time, in order to make a quick buck, many otherwise successful agents pick up bad habits, sink into depression, set themselves up for failure, and drop out of the field.

Keep in mind that your expenses are going to include not just those expenses you've always had. Now, you've actually got to put *more* money out. You have to dress well, you have to provide a clean car when showing properties, you might want to send out promotions, and so on.

I've never talked with a new agent who has been in the field for a year or so who didn't say he or she wished they had prepared with a bigger nest egg.

TRAP

The hard truth is that no matter how much you've got in reserve, it probably won't be quite enough.

On the other hand, if it's so tough the first few months, how does anyone survive?

The answer is perseverance. There's an old saying that I've always lived by that goes something like this: *Persistence is the key to success.* Keep at it and, one way or another, over time, you'll succeed. Yes, I know, it's the sort of thing that sounds good when someone else says it. But, in this case it's really true.

Truth 5: You Are in Competition with Everyone Else

It's important to understand that in a business, where reward is directly linked to productivity (you only get paid a commission when you make a deal), everyone is in competition with everyone else.

We're not talking about a deadly dog-eat-dog competition here. The vast majority of people selling real estate are friends—good people, the sort who would stop along the road to help someone with a flat tire.

Nevertheless, they are all looking for listings and buyers and deals. And every one of those that you get essentially means one that got away from them.

This is immediately obvious to some who are new to the field. But, for some reason it's a difficult concept for many other newcomers. If you're in this latter group, I'd like to address you: In this book in many places I talk about going to your broker for help, for teaming with another agent, for getting a mentor to help you get started. In all of those situations I'm suggesting you rely on someone else's experience, or judgment, or aid, or all of the above.

In other words, you can ask for and receive support from other agents. Some are very giving and will go out of their way to help a newcomer. Most will be willing to show you the ropes, to help you get started.

However, this can create a false impression that others in the field are dedicated to helping you get started, to providing you with the tools and ammunition you need. They are dedicated to getting sales and commissions, usually before all else, just like you. When helping you and making a commission for themselves conflict, which way do you think they'll jump?

TRAP

Remember, there's a difference between lending a helping hand and taking bread out of their mouths to put it in yours.

Of course, there are the ethics of the field. Besides the laws that you learn about when getting your license, you should also have learned ethics. Those rules we are particularly concerned with here involve stealing another agent's listings, buyers, and deals. Most real estate boards have specific rules covering these that you should learn and follow.

Nevertheless, the governing rule in real estate is that no matter with what agent you're dealing, in the back of your mind you must always remember that he or she is a competitor. That person wants to make a commission as badly as you do, perhaps more so.

That will help explain the sometimes strange behavior of your "friends" in the field—why they don't pass a lead onto you, why a written phone message happens to be garbled, why someone doesn't mention a new listing that's perfect for a buyer you have, and a hundred other nuances.

Remember, competition doesn't have to be nasty. Usually it isn't. Rather, it's more like friends shouldering each other to get to the dinner table. It's a big table, and there's plenty for everyone. Nevertheless, you're a competitor in a highly competitive field. Watch your back at all times.

TIP

Remember, no one is going to make money for you. You're in competition for that money with everyone else.

Truth 6: "Secret Agents" Don't Succeed

I find this the strangest truth of all. If you're going into real estate, why not tell everyone about it? Yet, many agents don't. They keep it to themselves.

Part of the reason that this is so may simply be the fact that, in most people's estimation among the general population, being a real estate agent is right up there with being a used car salesperson. Studies have repeatedly shown that, for whatever reason, the field is not held in high regard by the general public. (This fact may come as a shock to a few new agents who simply didn't realize it.)

In short, some who enter the field are slightly ashamed of it. If this is your attitude, then you might as well get out right now. You can't succeed unless you feel you are doing something worthwhile, which you are. Helping people find the home they want, sell their home, and thread through the maze of legal traps is a very admirable thing to do.

You're in a great profession. And when you step up to the plate and let others know that you're proud to be an agent, they'll be proud of you, too. I know one agent who's so happy to be in the field that she boasts about it right on her personalized license plate.

There may be a few in the field who are bad apples, but that's the case in every profession. The vast majority of agents are eager to do the right thing. When you tell others you're proud to be a real estate agent, you promote the entire field.

Thus, just about the time you decide to go into real estate you should begin forming a list of people whom you know who might be potential clients. This list should include

- Friends (close and distant)
- Relatives
- Workers from your previous job
- Neighbors
- People from social and service clubs
- Anyone else you can think of

Even before you get your license to sell, let all of them know you're going into real estate. Try to give them a heads up on approximately when you'll be ready to "hang out your shingle." Tell them that you're about to become the hottest real estate agent in town, and that you hope they'll think of only *you* when they decide to buy, sell, rent, or otherwise dabble in real estate.

If you can't do business with them yet, you can put them on notice that you're entering the field and that you hope (expect?) them to come to you with their business.

Do it early. Imagine your disappointment if the day after you get your license, you start telling your relatives that you're going into real estate, only to learn that your uncle listed his house the night before with someone else. "I'd have been thrilled to give you the listing," your uncle says, "But, I didn't even know you were going into real estate."

Don't keep it a secret. Let *everyone* know.

Truth 7: You Are Entirely Responsible for Your Own Success—or Failure

This is the biggest real estate truth of all.

Depending on what you do during your first year, you can eventually rise to the top. Or sink to the bottom. It's entirely up to you, and you can't blame it on anyone else.

Now, let's get on with seeing how you can become a *super-agent.*

3

First Things First: Find the Right Broker-Sponsor

Perhaps 80 percent of your ultimate success in real estate will be determined by the first office you sign on with. Get the right broker and your career could be made. Get the wrong broker and you could take a tumble from which it will be hard to recover.

How can there be a "right" or a "wrong" broker?

Easy—some fits are made in heaven ... and some in the other place. It would be a mistake to simply sign on with the first office that offers to sponsor you. The broker might not have time to spend with you. The office might have no training program. It might not be active enough to provide you with leads. And so on.

We're going to see what you need to look for in a broker-sponsor. But first, let's look at it the other way round.

TIP

Chances are that if you're starting out, you're going to be a salesperson working for a broker. (The exception would be in some states when you already have a college degree in a related field, such as a law degree. In such a case, you would be able to enter the profession as a full-fledged broker.) There's nothing wrong with starting as an apprentice. It's how the vast majority of us got started; the experience you get will be invaluable in preparing you for your later and, it is hoped, highly successful years.

Why Would a Broker Want You?

Take a moment and consider the profession of real estate from a broker-manager's perspective. (The broker may be the office owner or a manager for a franchise.) What is the broker looking for in a salesperson?

Productivity

If you haven't heard the term before, it's going to come up a lot as soon as you get on board: productivity. You're in the sales business, and, while there may not be a quota for deals, each salesperson is expected to be productive. That means bringing in listings and sales. The broker is looking for agents who can "produce."

In one sense, that means experienced agents, those who have shown year in and year out that they can bring in the deals. However, having experienced agents usually means that the commission split is less favorable to the broker. In order to keep experienced agents, the broker must often offer them 75 percent or more of each commission the agents make. In some cases, the agents only pay for desk space.

On the other hand, a brand new agent who is productive typically gets only 50 percent of each commission he or she brings in. In other words, as a new agent, you can actually be more valuable to a broker than an experienced agent—providing, of course, that you produce.

Churn and Burn

Therein lies the rub. Brokers know that new agents typically don't produce well until about their third year in the business. The exception is the first six months.

Agents who come into the business will typically try to list and sell homes to their relatives, friends, and associates. If the agent has a lot of relatives, friends, and associates who want to buy and sell, this *can* mean three to six deals in the first six months. And, of course, the broker takes half the commission earned out of each.

After this initial spurt of energy, the agent may languish with few listings and sales for a long period of time, perhaps a year or more. Brokers are aware of this pattern and some do a "churn and burn."

These offices hire lots of new agents all the time. They are looking for those initial deals that the agents bring in. Then, when the slow period hits, the broker sympathizes and points out that unless the agent continues to produce, she can't afford to keep him on. After all, the broker has all those expenses—rent, advertising, utilities, and so on.

It makes quite a good case, and the poor agent must now either sink or swim. Unfortunately, because of the nature of the business, most agents in this kind of situation sink. They leave the office, perhaps the profession. And then the broker brings in another bunch of newcomers and the pattern repeats.

It's important to understand that I'm not speaking of all brokers or all offices here, just a few. However, this typifies the kind of situation you want to avoid.

You want a broker who's building for the long haul. You want a broker who plans on helping you so that down the road you can help him or her.

Checking Out the Office

Your search for a broker-sponsor may begin casually when a friend says you'd be perfect for real estate and knows just the broker for you. You waltz in the office, sign a few papers, and soon you're sitting for the test. Unfortunately, that's probably the worst way to choose an office.

TIP

Remember, the office you select is, you hope, going to be your home for the foreseeable future, so it pays to make your selection carefully and wisely.

Here's how to select the right office ... and the right broker. Try beginning with the physical aspects.

Questions to Ask Yourself About the Office

- *Is It in a Good Location?* Most offices do not rely heavily on walk-in traffic anymore, but being in a strip mall or heavily trafficked street can be a plus, particularly when you're "up" for floor time. Of more concern is that the office is located near to your home and where you want to be selling real estate. A long commute or an office away from neighborhoods where you want to specialize is a definite no-no.

- *Is There Ample Parking?* Sounds like a no-brainer, but don't overlook the importance of parking. A new client who drives around the block twice and can't find a parking spot might just decide to go with a different agent.

- *Is It Attractive?* You don't need the Taj Mahal, but an orderly, attractive office that says "welcome" will help put your clients into the right mind-set even before you meet them.

- *Is It Busy Inside?* You want the office to hum with activity. No, it shouldn't be loud as a buzz saw, which would indicate it isn't big enough for all the agents, or as quiet as a tomb, which would show there's nothing happening. A level of busyness somewhere in between these two extremes signifies a healthy business.

TIP

I once had a broker who said, "Never trust an agent with a clean desk or an office that isn't messy." It's good advice for both agents and clients.

Checking Out the Web Site

It would be a real mistake to believe that you can operate today without the Web. Virtually all listings, including most listings for sale by owners (FSBOs), are on the Web. An increasing percentage of buyers check out listings on the Web *before* consulting an agent. And in the future, the key to sales may rely almost entirely on a Web-based business. Therefore, having a progressive office with an active Web presence is mandatory.

Having a Web presence is simple enough to do. If the office is Internet-savvy, it will let you know its Web address right on its signs. Simply go there.

Be sure to see if the actual office you're considering has its own site, or whether the office is simply operating under the umbrella of the franchise. Since you'll soon want to set up your own Web presence (see Chapter 10), you'll want to pay particular attention to see if every agent in the office has their own Web page.

Checking Out the Activity

People talk a lot. That can be of benefit to you.

Talk to one or two of the agents from an office under consideration. Ask them how active the place is. How many deals do they run a month? (You'll also ask the broker this question later on, when you interview, but at this point you're just scouting out possibilities.) The agents may not know the exact answer, but they should have a pretty good estimate. At least one deal per month per agent suggests an active office.

They should also be able to shed some light on the makeup of the agents who work there. How many work full-time? How many part-time? The more full-time agents, the better.

TRAP

You may plan to work part-time getting started, and this is an option in many offices. But, chances are, you won't be asked to move into an active office unless you're going to be an active agent.

Checking Out the Format

You'll want to know what kind of service the office offers. The following are the usual options.

- *Full-service.* You'll be asked to provide everything for your clients from finding buyers/sellers, to handling all the paperwork, to the closing. Of course, for that you'll expect to receive a full commission (minus your split and any franchise fee).

- *Discount.* The office may be full service, but more likely it will offer limited service. For example, the client may be asked to pay for some advertising. In such a case, the commission would also be reduced. Indeed, in some discount offices you won't work for a commission but instead may be salaried. Many say that discount brokerage is the wave of the future. That prediction, however, hasn't been proven as of this writing.

- *Independent.* With this type of office, the broker typically runs the place. It could be small, with only a few desks, or big, with dozens of agents. The advantage with an independent office is that you usually have lots of freedom in the type of deals, commission structure, and other aspects of the business.

- *Franchise.* Increasingly, offices are becoming part of a national franchise. Being part of one gives you the advantage of national recognition (you represent Coldwell Banker, or Prudential, or Century 21, or whomever). In addition, there are often impressive training programs and sometimes even mentoring programs for new agents. On the other hand, you will probably be asked to bend to the policies of the office. You'll have less freedom in negotiations with your clients, and you even may have to follow a particular dress code.

- *Buyer's office.* This type of office has few listings. Instead, it concentrates on finding buyers and closing deals. It's often easier to get started in this office because there are usually lots of leads. However, over time it may be harder to sustain the business.

- *Listing office.* This type of office concentrates on signing a lot of listings and letting other offices handle the sales. Over the long haul, it should do well. Usually the best office has a good balance between listings and sales.

TIP

One sign of a healthy office is when the agents have lots of listings and sell most of those listings themselves.

Your Interview from the Broker's Perspective

Once you find an office that appears right for you, you're going to need to interview with the broker. Essentially, you'll be asking for a job.

Don't expect every broker or office to welcome you with open arms. Some brokers may be grumpy and simply say they don't have time for new agents. Others may indicate a lack of desk space. Yet other brokers or offices may simply tell you to turn in your résumé and they'll call you.

Don't get discouraged. There are no lack of real estate offices and brokers around. If your ideal broker/office isn't interested in you, someone else may be. And you may end up with an even better match than if you had gone with your first choice.

Be sure you have a dynamite résumé, and come prepared for the interview. Consider this the same as interviewing for any other job.

TIP

One helpful way to prepare for the interview is role reversal. Ask yourself, what is the broker looking for in a new agent? The answer, it is hoped, will be you. If not, why not?

By anticipating what the broker will be looking for, you can prepare yourself better for the initial interview. Brokers look for different things in a new agent. The following were what I looked for when I was picking salespeople.

What Brokers Look For

- *Gregariousness.* Likes to talk, mix, and work with people and help solve their problems. The broker may ask you to tell a few stories about yourself interacting with others.

- *Ability to be a good listener.* You won't do well in real estate unless you can hear what people are telling you. Listen to what the broker says and don't jump on his words to respond.

- *Having an easy and comfortable way about them.* I figure that most new agents can learn the paperwork and other details. Try to impress with the fact that you're proud of the profession.

- *Spark plug.* Show that you're a person who is a self-starter, who can come in each morning and get going without a pep talk.

- *Maturity.* Chronological age doesn't matter. Some people in their fifties act like children, and some in their twenties act like adults and are emotionally stable. It's hard to hide or change this.

- *Honesty.* I would never work with a person who I felt wouldn't do the right thing. If a broker asks an ethics question, think carefully before answering.

- *Preparedness.* Show you know what's involved in getting into real estate and are financially and emotionally prepared for it.

As mentioned, brokers may be looking to see if you have some choice listings you will bring with you. If this is the main thrust of the broker's concern, then I'd be very suspicious of his or her intentions over the long haul. It just might turn out to be that the broker needs you more than you need him or her!

Your Interview from Your Perspective

You should come away from your interview with a broker with specific information that will help you make your decision. Remember, signing up isn't a one-way street. You're interviewing your broker at the same time he or she is interviewing you.

The following are questions you should ask your broker. Explanations follow.

What You Should Ask the Broker

- What's your policy on retention of new agents?
- How long have you been in business, and what is the market share?
- How many agents do you have, and what is their experience?
- What is the commission split?
- Is there a written office policy?
- Is there a training program?
- Where will I have my desk?
- Will I have floor time?
- Does the office have a secretary?
- Will I have a computer?
- Do you offer a relocation referral program?
- Will I be an employee or independent contractor?
- Do you have a health insurance plan?

- Do you carry errors and omissions (e&o) insurance?
- Is everyone in the office a Realtor?
- Which of my expenses will you pay for?

Your Expenses or Will Broker Pay?

Course to pass test	$_____	[ ]
License test	$_____	[ ]
Realtor associate dues	$_____	[ ]
Business cards	$_____	[ ]
Listing signs	$_____	[ ]
Lock boxes	$_____	[ ]
MLS input (Listing fees)	$_____	[ ]
Health insurance	$_____	[ ]
E&O insurance	$_____	[ ]

What's your policy on rentention of new agents?

Basically, you want to know how you'll be treated. What if you don't bring in a lot of listings or deals right away? What's the turnover rate? How many new agents a year does the office go through? The answers will give you an opportunity to size up your chances with this outfit.

How long have you been in business, and what is the market share?

Generally speaking, longevity suggests a stable business. On the other hand, sometimes a new office just getting started will offer more opportunities. Also ask what's the market share of this office. If there are 40 offices in the area and this one captures 10 percent of the market, that's good. If there are four offices in the area and the market share is 10 percent, that's not so good.

How many agents do you have, and what is their experience?

Just as in atomic energy, there's a minimum amount of mass needed to produce a chain reaction. You want enough agents in the office so that you can bounce listings, deals, and ideas off one another and in doing so create even more business. Also, you want a variety of specialties including not only residential but also commercial and office space as well. This will help you, over time, to experience other aspects of the real estate business.

TIP

Usually a good active office will have between 8 and 15 agents. Any less, and there simply may not be enough coverage. Any more, and you may end up stepping on one another's toes.

What is the commission split?

You can expect 50-50. That means that the broker will take half of everything you earn.

While that may seem a lot, remember that the broker is footing the bill (or should be) for your desk space, phone, advertising, and a dozen other expenses. As you get more experience and your productivity grows, you will want to adjust the split more in your favor. However, when you do that you may be asked to shoulder more of the expenses.

There may also be a franchise fee that will come out of the commission, typically 6 percent. And the office may charge an administrative fee (to cover paperwork and processing) of several hundred dollars on top of the commission, paid by the client directly to the broker. Some top agents have even begun charging their own administrative fees.

Is there a written office policy?

All good offices will have a written office policy. It protects your rights by setting out policy for many different situations. This document will keep decisions from being made in an arbitrary and capricious manner. For example, suppose you have a dispute with another agent; just check to see what the policy is regarding resolution. A good office will have a policy book that will be given to you. It will also explain many of the ethics that the broker emphasizes. You should read this information carefully so you understand how the office operates.

Is there a training program?

As a new agent, I wouldn't sign on to an office that didn't offer a training program. This is what will propel you into the business.

Be sure to also ask how long the program lasts. (Months are better than weeks.) How intensive is it? (It should meet at least three times a week.) Does it include orientation for new agents? (Without this session, you're on your own to figure out who's who and what's going on.)

Where will I have my desk?

Forget a private office. As a new agent, chances are you'll get a desk and, if you're lucky, a cubicle. You'll be out there in the center of the office in the "bullpen" along with most of the other new agents.

But it won't be so bad. Most modern offices have several conference rooms where you can take meetings with your clients. They'll never see where you actually work.

TRAP

Some new agents, particularly those coming from other professions, have a hard time being dumped down in the middle of a large office space with other agents. My suggestion is that you try to live with your desk space. Remember, you'll only be using it for research on properties, to access your computer, and to handle office work. Your real job is out there in the field taking listings, showing buyers around, and so on.

Will I have floor time?

This is an opportunity to be "up" when a client walks in over the transom and asks to see any agent. You're the one who will come forward to speak for the office.

For new agents it's a great opportunity to get leads. More experienced agents are usually happy to give up their floor time since they already have lots of leads and need the time to work them.

Does the office have a secretary?

The secretary's job may actually be that of a receptionist who also does some secretarial work such as making copies or writing letters. A real estate office that doesn't have a receptionist usually looks impoverished to clients. They expect to be "received" when they enter, so it's an important function.

Ask if you'll be able to use the secretarial services on occasion. It may be that the secretary is strictly for the broker's benefit.

Will I have a computer?

I wouldn't work for an office that didn't provide a computer terminal at my desk. Today, in almost every area of the country, listings are available through a computerized service. You can also find all sorts of valuable information online. Increasingly, a computer is an essential part of the business.

Also ask what program is being used for accessing real estate and how difficult or easy it is to access the multiple listing service (MLS) with it. The broker may beam and proudly talk about how good the program is, or sort of chuckle and say that in spite of it, people get by. You don't want a program that fights you all the way. (See also Chapter 10.)

Do you offer a relocation referral program?

This can be another source of leads (see Chapter 7). It will cost you part of your commission if you accept a referral and get a sale. But, then again, that's a sale that you wouldn't otherwise have made.

Will I be an employee or an independent contractor?

Ninety-five percent of salespeople in real estate are "independent contractors." That means that you essentially work for yourself. It is a legal term. According to the Internal Revenue Service (IRS), you work for someone else, but technically you are not an employee. (That means you're responsible for paying your own taxes.)

It also means that your "employer" won't take out deductions for payroll tax, contributions to Social Security under the Federal Insurance Contributions Act (FICA), and probably not worker's comp (although many offices do, in fact, carry this). You also won't be entitled to benefits including vacation time, health benefits, or severance pay.

Yes, you'll have to answer to your broker, who is entrusted with your supervision through the real estate licensing laws of your state. On the other hand, how you achieve your listings and sales is largely your own affair, provided you don't do anything illegal or unethical.

TIP

In a few offices, the agents are employees. They are salaried instead of commissioned and have the usual employee rights and benefits under the laws of your state.

Do you have a health insurance plan?

In your previous employment, your employer might have provided you with health coverage. Here, as an independent contractor, you'll probably be responsible for it on your own.

However, getting individual health coverage, particularly as we grow older or have illnesses, becomes increasingly difficult. So, it may be very important to you to find out if your broker offers a health plan and, if so, how much it costs and whether you can buy into it. Also, find out how long you have to work for the office before the plan kicks in.

For some older agents just starting out, this may be the single most important question.

Do you carry errors and omissions (E&O) insurance?

Errors and omissions insurance, or E&O, covers you in case a client sues you. It's important in all businesses and particularly so in real estate where clients tend to be highly litigious. Without it, you could be sued for your actions and potentially lose all of your assets.

TRAP

Don't think you can get by without E&O insurance because you'll be careful and always do a good job. In real estate you're almost always working with other agents. If the other agent screws up on a deal, the buyer or seller will sue everyone involved. Thus, even if ultimately you're not culpable, you still need insurance to cover your attorney's costs as well as any settlements against you.

I would not work for an office that did not have E&O insurance.

Is everyone in the office a Realtor?

It comes down to professionalism. You become a Realtor by joining The National Association of Realtors, the biggest trade organization in the field. It established the original "Code of Ethics" years ago. It promotes a real estate agency, provides courses of improvement, holds national conferences, offers lobbyists to advocate agent's causes, and much more. You can be an agent without being a Realtor (broker member) or Realtor Associate (salesperson member), but why would anyone want to? The top brokers in the field almost universally are Realtors. It is a label of distinction and quality. Most new agents quickly join up as associates.

If someone in the office isn't a Realtor, you should ask why? Were they booted out of the organization for unbecoming conduct? If so, why are they still employed in the office? It's something to consider.

Which of my expenses will you pay for?

You will have a lot of expenses when starting out in real estate. However, usually depending on how eager the broker is to get you, the office may pay some of them.

Finding a Mentor

Much has been made in real estate about the importance of having a mentor when you're getting started. A mentor is someone who will guide you through the early stages of your career. If your mentor is good, he or she can help you avoid many pitfalls and traps while at the same time tipping you off to tricks of the trade that you might otherwise take years to discover on your own. Obviously, having a mentor is a good thing.

On the other hand, most new real estate agents don't have mentors and many still succeed. Rather, they piece together what they need to know from experiences with other agents—some good, and some not so good. While it is not necessary to have a mentor in order to succeed, it can be helpful.

TIP

Many offices offer mentoring experiences for new agents. For example, you may be invited to go on listing presentations three times with three different experienced agents. Quite frankly, you'll learn far more this way than going on three presentations with the same one experienced agent.

If you want a true mentor, it's up to you to pick the person and then to get her or him to agree to coach and guide you. The problem, of course, is that many top agents simply don't have the time or the desire to take on a mentee.

TRAP

Many new agents think of a mentor in the Asian tradition where you sit at the feet for a master for years and learn everything he can teach. This approach is both good and bad. You will learn all of the Master's good traits as well as all of his bad ones. Better you think of a mentor as simply a coach whom you can talk with about how you're doing, what your goals are, and where you go from here.

What Should You Look for in a Mentor?

Above all, most newcomers want someone who is successful in real estate, a *super-agent*, an agent who's making millions. After all, why would you want a mentor who was a failure?

This is short-sighted. A *super-agent* may indeed be able to show you some of the tricks of the trade. But, on the other hand, any agent who's been around a while and who has done so making a good income can also do that.

What's more important is that you can "open up" with a mentor. You're going to have all sorts of questions from day one and you probably won't to be able find anyone to answer them all. Your broker is going to be too busy to sit down with you on a daily (or in some cases even a weekly) basis for heart-to-heart talks. A trainer might have more time, but then you'll be competing with all the other new agents for the trainer's attention.

My suggestion for an ideal mentor is an older agent who has made his or her big money in real estate and is now in the office still being productive but not pushing as hard as in earlier days. This person might indeed be willing to take a new agent under his or her wing. Many people in this position feel the need to pay back some of the benefits they've received from real estate. You could be as much an opportunity for them as they are for you.

What to Avoid in a Mentor

You don't want a mentor with whom you don't hit it off. You'll find it hard to talk with this person and, as a result, the benefits will be limited.

You don't want a mentor who wants something financial from you. Some experienced agents will agree to mentor you for a cut of your commissions. While there's nothing wrong with this approach, the financial arrangements tend to sour the relationship. On the other hand, a mentor may ask for your help, as, for example, sitting on his or her Open House. This can benefit both of you.

You don't want a mentor who is too busy for you.

TRAP

I once knew an agent whose mentor was his broker. He would sometimes sit for hours outside the broker's office waiting to talk with him. Once, he even called in on an outside line pretending to be someone from an escrow company, just so he could get his mentor's attention and ask a question. This wasn't a mentor. It was a failed hope.

You don't want a mentor who doesn't have high ethical standards, no matter how successful this person may appear to be. In the long run, an unethical agent *always* runs into trouble.

How Do You Ask to Be Mentored?

If mentoring is part of your in-house training, it's easy. Certain experienced agents will be designated as mentors, and you simply ask who that person is. They will probably want to engage you in a conversation to see what your goals are, how prepared you are for the field, and how determined you are to succeed. If it all pans out to their liking, you've got your mentor.

It's more difficult in a less formal situation. You may have to arrange to meet the person who you want to be your mentor over coffee and become friends with him or her, first. When you finally pop the question about mentoring, he or she may be standoffish, or otherwise unwilling, so don't preclude rejection.

On the other hand, persistence usually pays off. If you keep coming back, particularly if you can impress him or her with your determination to succeed, he or she may eventually agree.

What If You Can't Find a Mentor?

As I noted, while a mentor is desirable, it's not absolutely necessary. A great many agents have reached the top by pulling themselves up by their own bootstraps.

Some people have not just one mentor, but many of them. They make friends with all of the older, more experienced agents in the office. Perhaps they bring them coffee or engage them in conversations about a particularly troubling deal. Along the way, they get the help, if not the direct coaching, that they need.

What Else Do You Need to Learn Immediately?

Finally, let's consider two items that you'll need to add to your repertoire from the very beginning. These are the *listing agreement* and the *deposit receipt* (also called the *purchase agreement*).

When you study for your license, you should learn the basics about filling these two vital forms out. However, that's not going to be much help when you're out in the field. You can't really bring along your textbook and keep referring to it while working with the forms that are the basics of your trade.

So, get some forms from your office and ask your mentor or another experienced agent to help you in filling them out. Use a pretend deal and keep changing the situation (price, terms, contingencies, and so on) so that eventually you can fill out the forms in your sleep.

You need to find time to do this while you're learning everything else. Consider it an essential part of your "first things first" education.

4

All You Have Is Your Time

There's nothing more intimidating or exhilarating than the sound of an alarm clock the morning of your first day of a new career. It buzzes with the combined excitement and fear that makes an adventure out of starting anything new. Yet, with the right attitude and the correct set of skills, getting up in the morning will be nothing less than the beginning of your dream as a top real estate agent.

Unlike other jobs in which you are explicitly told when and where to go each day, there is no "norm" in real estate. One day may be spent in the car showing potential buyers properties around town while another is spent entirely behind your desk answering calls or filling out paperwork. Often you may not know what the day will bring even as you're sipping the morning coffee. Clearly, flexibility is key in managing your career.

While the allure of a flexible make-your-own-hours lifestyle initially drives many into real estate, it can be easy to fall into a time-wasting rut. After all, spending hours surfing online, shopping, running errands, or any of a million other distractions can instantly derail your efforts. Compound these distractions with the lack of immediate supervision and it's easy to see how time can slip through your fingers. In order to be successful in the face of an ambiguous schedule, you must be disciplined.

One of the most important lessons a beginning real estate agent can learn is how to manage his or her time. The schedule you keep will go a long way toward dictating the money you earn. The following are several simple tips (and a few traps) that can help you best manage your greatest asset—time.

TIP

A real estate agent's time and commission are intertwined. As you begin your career, treat your time as if it were more precious than money. Spend each moment investing in yourself, and you eventually will see the monetary reward.

Know Thyself

There is a great lesson to be learned by simply observing people at work. One person has his headphones on and the music is so loud it's audible to the passersby. Another is buried in pink Post-it notes scribbling madly, while a third person is surrounded by the remnants of several mornings' breakfast and hard at work on the phone. It doesn't take long to learn the lesson: Everyone has her or his own style.

It would be a mistake to simply try to copy someone else's habits and expect the same results. What works for her may not work for you. The first step in managing your time is figuring out in which environment you work best.

TRAP

There is no one correct way to organize your time. The savvy real estate agent will seek out methods that will work well with his or her style rather than trying to find a "silver bullet" answer.

Below are several questions to help get you started thinking about your own style and how to best manage your time.

Where Do I Work Most Efficiently?

As we know by now, real estate agents split time across a number of tasks and a variety of locations. But not everyone works efficiently in all scenarios. Are you the type of person who can still get things done on a cell phone while farming a neighborhood? Can you handle taking calls from your clients while you are away from your desk? Think carefully about where you would be most efficient accomplishing the various tasks that you need to do. It may make sense to limit your time in the field and spend more time behind your desk so that you have the necessary resources available at your fingertips. Or the other way round.

What Are My Biggest Distractions?

Technology has made all our lives a little bit more complicated. The cell phone has become an appendage for a successful real estate agent. But there is a downside to too many tech gadgets: distraction. If you are the type of person who can't check listings online without also going to a sports Web site or can't take a call on the cell phone without also calling a friend, consider constraints. Limit yourself to checking e-mail in the morning, after lunch, and at the end of the day. Only make personal calls after work or during breaks. It is important to know the level of discipline you need to self-inflict to make sure you do not become too distracted on the job.

TRAP

Working from home may sound like the answer, but it is not for everyone. There are so many distractions when trying to get stuff done from your living room that it may be impossible to actually accomplish anything. Be very careful before you try this, and make sure you take "sanity checks" every once in a while to make sure you are being as productive as you can be.

What Will It Take to Be Satisfied at the End of the Day?

Naturally, getting a commission check tends to make everyone satisfied. But, you're not likely to get one of those every day. Yet, you'll be going to work most days.

Everyone has internal goals, and feeling satisfied at the end of the day indicates you've met yours. Your goal may simply be talking to three clients. Or making 30 cold calls. Or checking out a dozen properties. Or ...? What gives you satisfaction? What makes you feel that you've done a good and thorough job? It is very important to know what it will take to make you satisfied at the end of the day. That way you can set goals that will make you productive.

What Do I Do When I Don't Have Anything to Do?

Idle hands do not make the real estate agent money. There should be no such thing as downtime on the job. You may be waiting to hear about an offer you made or simply entering a stagnant period of little activity, but you should never have nothing to do. It is extremely important to maximize your time during these slower periods. This is precious time.

Know yourself, and know what it is that you need to work on. We all have developmental areas, and successful agents will continually try to improve in these areas when the opportunity presents itself.

Answering the questions above will help you narrow down the type of work environment that is likely to work best for you. Remember, there is no one right answer, and we may change our style from time to time.

Now that we have a good idea of the type of environment that may work best for your style, it is time to consider the type of game face you need to wear while on the job. To do this, we turn to the Stage Matrix.

The Stage Matrix

Over the years, I have seen a myriad of time management styles. Some of the same things that worked for a successful agent sunk the person at the next desk. The key takeaway from my observations is that you must maximize your time by working with *your* key strengths.

Some people have a rare skill that will be a strength for them throughout their career. (For example, a person who is able to speak several languages fluently.) For most of us, however, the real strength in our skill set comes from knowing how we can take advantage of common abilities.

The set of capabilities shared by most successful real estate agents is quite long. Just about everyone in the trade should be able to perform basic financial calculations and balance work for multiple clients. However, not everyone maximizes their use of these common skills.

From years of experience and observations, I have compiled a matrix consisting of two dimensions which highly differentiate between the successful and the average real estate agent. By knowing where you fall in the matrix (a medium, an atmosphere, an environment, a place in which you live and work.), you will be able to better tailor your time and your skills. I refer to this construct as the "Stage Matrix" because your behavior on stage and in the spot light (e.g. in front of the client, your broker, etc.) will be dictated by where you fall in the matrix.

Setting the Stage

There are two key dimensions in the Stage Matrix. First, on the Y-axis, is your level of extroversion versus introversion. (There are a host of tests you can take to figure out if you are an introvert or an extrovert, but for the purposes of this example, we'll keep it simple.) An extrovert enjoys and seeks out interaction with others, while the introvert prefers to work alone and is quiet by comparison. It is not necessarily better to be introverted or extroverted, but each style demands different tactics.

On the *X* axis is the scale between calculated and spontaneous. Clearly these two traits are opposites and most of us will have a bit of each. However, there is likely one side pulling more weight than the other, suggesting that you, generally speaking, prefer to plan things or fly by the seat of your pants.

Table 4.1   The Stage Matrix

	Calculated	Spontaneous
Extroverted	Captain	Entertainer
Introverted	Thinker	Artist

Now plot yourself along these two dimensions and see where you lie.

- *Captain.* You enjoy meeting and working with all kinds of people, and you run a tight ship. Your office is tidy, and your scheduler is your best friend. Too many clients may overload you. Do not overlook your administrative obligations.

- *Entertainer.* You are a people person. You are great at capturing new leads and enjoy showing houses. Be careful not to miss important dates (a scheduler would help), and remember, patience is a virtue.

- *Thinker.* You are a heads-down type of person. You enjoy working at your computer and prefer to correspond via e-mail. Remember to give your clients enough attention, and don't be afraid to use the phone.

- *Artist.* You are creative and can roll with the punches. Use your creativity to differentiate yourself from other agents. Remember, some people may have a hard time reading you, so be explicit and "use your words."

It becomes fairly evident that where you fall in the Stage Matrix will dramatically influence the ways in which you should focus your time and energy. This isn't to say that one type is better than the next, but that each requires a unique strategy to ensure success as a real estate agent. Focus on what may work best for you as we continue to discuss specific activities of the successful real estate agent.

TIP

 A helpful exercise is evaluating personality strengths and weaknesses. Consider two traits, and try to plot them in a matrix like the one above. Now work to figure out a set of qualities that are unique to each quadrant. In this manner, you can not only learn more about yourself but also help understand the behaviors and attitudes of others around you.

How Big a Pie?

Now that we have spent some time discussing the type of person you are and your stage presence, it's time to trigger the assets. We all have limited resources and can only do so much in a given day. How should you spend your fuel?

Let's consider a pie that represents the total amount of time you have to devote to your job. From person to person, there will be many things that change the makeup of this pie. For example, the amount of time spent working will differ dramatically. According to the National Association of Realtors (NAR), the typical Realtor spends about 46 hours working per week. This may or may not seem reasonable to you. How big is your pie?

Once you know the number of hours you expect to work per week (e.g., the size of your pie), let's consider how to slice up the time. Generally speaking, there are several high-level tasks that consume a majority of the successful real estate agent's time:

Slices of the Pie

- *Marketing.* Real estate agents normally get paid only if they close a transaction. Therefore, an agent's job inherently hinges on the ability to continually bring in clients. Marketing is key for driving new business. The more time spent marketing up front, the more chances you have of making big money down the road.

- *Leads.* The outcome of any marketing campaign will be leads. We will talk about leads later in the book, but for now let's simply refer to them as potential clients. In other words, as a result of your marketing efforts, you have the names and contact information for people who may be interested in making a real estate transaction.

- *Online.* The Internet is a very powerful tool in the real estate agent's arsenal. Depending on your comfort and interest levels, you can spend anywhere from 5 to 60 percent of your time online. This time may be spent flipping through virtual listing books or managing a custom Web site. The scope of your online presence may vary dramatically, but it can be very costly in terms of lost business for an agent to avoid the Web entirely.

- *Training.* There will always be new things for you to learn. These can range from tax codes to computer programs. Complacency will limit your ability to grow your knowledge (often a direct corollary to the growth of your wallet).

TIP

Education is the best investment you can make. Take the time to learn all you can about successful agent tricks, tax codes, computer programs, and anything else that will give you an edge. The time spent now will likely turn to financial dividends down the road.

- *Paperwork.* After successfully hooking clients, you will likely need to complete several different documents in order to facilitate the deal. You should definitely consider time spent on enhancing your understanding of contracts as a major component on the new agent's time clock. (The first two that any agent will likely want to focus on are the listing agreement and deposit receipt.) Tracking escrow documents is also an important use of time.

- *Administration.* As with any job, there will be a variable amount of administration work to be done. This can range from managing benefits to filling in timesheets. While this slice will differ dramatically, depending on the office you decide to join, it will never entirely disappear.

- *Follow-up.* The funny thing about real estate is that people never disappear, they just lie dormant. So, for example, the couple you sold a house to five years ago, may now be deciding to move to a larger home. Guess who they're going to call first? It is very important to stay in contact with past clients and to make sure they have you in the back of their mind in case it comes time to make another property move.

- *Volunteering.* Goodwill is very useful as a real estate agent. The reason is simple: You are, in many ways, selling your image to clients. This image includes your attitude, expertise, time, and everything else that a client may ask you to provide during a transaction. For this reason (if not for moral reasons), volunteering is very important. You can engage in community events (also another good way to generate leads) or you can volunteer around the office and help a fellow agent hold an open house. The point is that good habits like volunteering will pay back in a magnitude greater than their cost.

Remember that these slices are not mutually exclusive or collectively exhaustive. You should not limit yourself to these activities, but definitely make sure you are spending an appropriate amount of time driving your career in the right direction.

Now that we have discussed several different slices, let's see how the pie may look during different stages of your career.

On Your First Day

Your first day on the job probably will be filled with questions and searching. You'll undoubtedly want to find out where all the paper supplies are kept, how to operate the copy machine, and so on. You'll also probably find yourself set up for a training program (although the program may not necessarily start immediately). Keep in mind that this first day will be both the easiest and the most difficult to get through. It's the easiest because you have only one task to perform: make a good impression. It's the most difficult because you only get one chance. Your pie on this day will look quite strange, as marketing yourself will consume almost all of your time.

The fact remains: a first impression sticks. When beginning your new agent's job, you will have a chance to walk around the office and meet all the people whom you will be working with (at least all the ones on that day). You'll probably be introduced to the person who will handle your training as well as other staff including a mortgage broker, someone who handles escrows, and maybe a closer. It is critical to get off on the right foot because these people will quickly become your

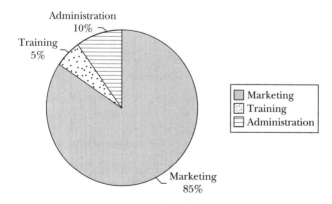

Figure 4.1 Productivity Pie—On Your First Day

first-line resource network. They will get you going through the early days and show you all the tricks you need to know. So, shake off the jitters and quiet the butterflies in your stomach, it's time to go to work.

Put on a Smile

The fact of the matter is that there is tremendous power in a smile. For proof of this, consider your own experiences. Have you ever met someone who shook your hand, made eye contact, and did everything else that seems cordial except smile? If yes, you probably thought suspiciously of this person. What is she hiding? Conversely, someone who may miss your hand when going for a shake or crack her voice nervously during introductions can instantly be forgiven with a single smile.

TIP

Smile. It's a powerful tool, it's totally free, it's easy... do it!

Remembering Names

I remember my first day working in a large office. As I walked around and met everyone, I couldn't help but be slightly intimidated by the sheer number of people under the same roof. Naturally, I couldn't remember which name matched with which face and throughout the day I would greet people with a generic "hey." It seemed many had already forgotten my name too. However, there was one person who constantly called me by my first name. I must have run into him three or four times and he never failed to remember my name while I simply returned my generic "hey." Before long, I was forced to remember his name just so it didn't seem strange when he called me by mine. And so I learned a valuable lesson; if you want people to remember your name, remember theirs.

"But I'm so bad at remembering people's names!" I hear this response almost instantly when advising people to learn names as soon as possible. But this is usually nothing more than an excuse. Soon after you meet someone, write down his or her name. If it helps, you can even draw out the physical layout of the office and put people's names in their respective spots. In this manner, you can create a cheat sheet. Remember, names can be work but it is certainly time well spent.

Earning Personal Capital

If location, location, location are the three most important factors in real property, impression, impression, impression are the three for people. You always want to be conscious of the impression you are making. This is true for all salespersons. As a result, it is very important to hit the ground running. You want to make a great early impression to earn capital that will help you later in your career.

You can earn capital by doing a great job in your days on the job. Be prepared to spend extra hours in the office learning the computer systems or talking with colleagues. Whatever you can do, let people know that you are destined to be a top-producing agent.

Now What? (Your First Month)

Twenty-four hours after you begin your new career as a real estate agent, it's already time to get serious. The name of the game is selling, and there is no time to waste. But where should you begin?

Don't expect to hit the ground running with several deals in the works. An exception may be if you have friends or family who are looking to make real estate transactions. But even in these circumstances, your pipeline of deals will only be so long.

The road to big commission paydays is paved with long hours of marketing, learning, and selling. Let's begin by revisiting the productivity pie.

Here, we can see quite clearly that over half of your time should be spent marketing and pursuing leads. Considering all the new people and tools you will be dealing with, spending 55 percent of your time chasing potential clients may seem like a huge effort. However, the time will be well spent. Remember, the sales cycle for a real estate transaction can take several months. That means that even if you hook a client today, you may not be able to spend your commission check for months. Can you afford to wait to build your client roster?

The next most important activity to focus on is training. It is very important that you learn the tools that will make you successful. Spending about 20 percent of your time in the near future will more than pay for itself down the road as you are able to whip up

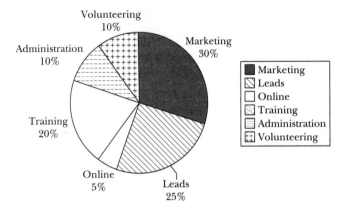

Figure 4.2   Productivity Pie—Your First Month

documents, zoom through computer applications, and process a ton of information easily because of your training.

One other, perhaps striking, activity to spend a lot of time on in the beginning is volunteering. While you should expect to be extremely busy in the early days of your career, in some respects you have more free time than you will later on because your time is spent at your own discretion. For this reason, it may be easier to volunteer now compared to when you have several different clients clamoring for your attention. Also, time spent volunteering will further help you to establish your professional identity. Your colleagues will quickly see the type of person you are, and your reputation will begin on a positive note.

TIP

Your professional brand will be a critical success factor in your career. It is extremely important to actively work on your image. Remember, there is a lot of "carry-over" in terms of your reputation. What you do now will stick with you for quite some time. Make sure you put the right foot forward early on.

Hitting Your Stride (Your First Year)

Once you have successfully navigated through the early going, you will likely hit your stride. This implies that you have found your way through the office, set up all of your equipment and marketing tools, and probably landed your first clients. Now it's time to shift gears slightly and begin earning your keep.

Let's begin again by taking a look at how the productivity pie might look once you've hit your stride.

In the chart, you can immediately see that every slice we mentioned previously is in play now. You have to be extremely agile and multitask throughout the day.

A major portion of your time should be spent pursuing leads. This activity will remain at the heart of most good real estate agents. It often takes several years before your Rolodex or personal digital assistant (PDA) is dense enough such that people will come to you when they need to sell a home rather than the other way around.

Intuition no doubt tells you that the amount of time spent on training will decrease as time goes on. This outcome is expected, because after a while you will have likely mastered most of the common tools and techniques necessary to perform 80 percent of your job. But do not stop trying to learn new things. Training should always be ongoing for the successful real estate agent, as you can never have too much knowledge or expertise.

Now you will begin to spend a sizable amount of time tracking deals that you have signed but have not yet closed. Also, your online time will go up as you invariably are spending time managing your own Web site, looking up listings, corresponding with clients, and even searching for local information over the Web.

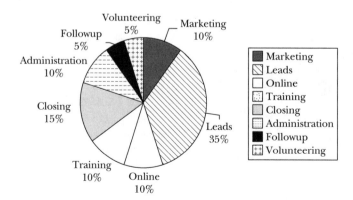

Figure 4.3 Productivity Pie—Your First Year

Things including administration, followup, and volunteering will eat up the remaining parts of your time. Although often considered less glamorous, these functions should not be overlooked, as they are critical in your growth.

Reach for Riches (Your First Business)

After several years in the real estate game, agents will likely think of themselves as running a small business. No longer are you an individual hustling for leads and struggling to connect the strings between deals. Now you likely have a résumé stacked with a number of successful transactions. In this scenario, your time dramatically shifts and you develop different priorities. Again, let's look at the same pie chart as used above.

Once again, the chart shows that marketing takes a very dominant part of your time. Compared to time spent marketing early in your career, the time spent marketing now differs in the respect that you are trying to market something slightly different. Depending on your business model, you will be selling many things other than your individual skills. For example, if you have other agents working with or for you, your marketing efforts are to bring people to the office, but it doesn't often matter who gets the deal. In this case, your objective is to market your office name. Other times, you may have a set of properties that you manage or otherwise have a vested interest. In this type of situation, you are trying to market your investment port-

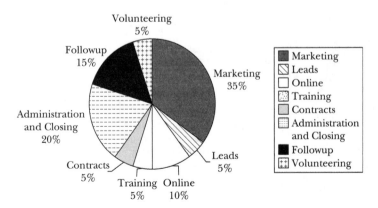

Figure 4.4 Productivity Pie—Your First Business

folio. The point is that your key strengths may change over time, and the goals of your marketing energies must change in synch.

It may come as no surprise that you will likely spend a large amount of time handling administrative duties as a business owner. These may include everything from hiring custodial staff to managing the office finances, to closings for others.

After such a long time in the game, you will likely have a fairly robust set of contacts. Therefore, following up with these contacts will require a sizable amount of time. Some of this time can be made up by the reduction in effort of chasing new leads. After all, leads are now coming to you!

Depending on your Web presence, you may be spending a significant amount of time online managing your own Web site. This effort is not required, but is becoming increasingly common. Also, contracts remain a small piece of the pie, as you will likely close a few deals but will commonly have people doing much of the work for you.

The Three Constants

Regardless of where you are in your career, there are three activities that should constantly be on your mind: goal setting, status checking, and visualization.

Goal Setting

It is very important to make sure that you set appropriate and achievable goals for each stage of your career. These goals can come in many forms and range from financial goals to the number of leads generated. There is no correct or standard goal that you should strive to achieve. However, it is imperative that you have both short-term and long-term goals.

- *Short-term goals.* These goals should be fairly easily attainable and should drive you toward your longer-term goals. It is much easier to achieve a long-term goal if you have a tactical plan—a series of small steps that will lead you to your ultimate objective.

- *Long-term goals.* What would it take for you to be happy? If you put in 40 hours a week for 50 weeks, you will have worked 40,000 hours by your twenty-first year in real estate. What do you want to show for it? Make sure you have set your long-term goals lofty enough to make all the time spent worth it.

Status Checking

How do you know if you're spending your time wisely? Sometimes, we get so caught up in the nitty-gritty that it's impossible to tell when we are wasting our efforts. Be sure to set up several checks and balances to ensure that you are making the most of your time.

The following are some questions you can ask yourself routinely as status checks.

Questions on Your Status

- Are my short-term goals congruent with my long-term goals?
- Have I achieved my short-term goals?
- On what piece of the productivity pie do I need to spend more time working?
- Am I being efficient?
- Am I happy?

While each question is important, the last one is the ultimate status check. If you are not happy, you will definitely want to change your situation. If you cannot see where the areas for improvement are, talk with someone. Your colleagues have likely been in a similar situation and can help steer you through the tough time. Also, reach to your friends and family to paint away the blues. Starting a new career (especially one as intense as real estate) can take a serious toll. Do not be afraid to reach for help if things are becoming too much.

Visualization

It is very hard to accomplish anything you cannot imagine; dare to dream big thoughts. Imagine what your life might be like once you achieve these goals. Do you drive a fancy car, live in a mansion, manage a dozen people? The dream will be different for each person and should be something both personal and meaningful.

Keep the visualization on your mind. Put a picture of the luxury car, house, or whatever your dream is on the side of your computer. During long days, this picture will help remind you why you are putting in the hard work and what it is that drives you.

The visualization may or may not eventually become a reality. However, only with a dream in mind will you make the most of the reality. (And realty for that matter!)

5

1-2-3 to Getting Leads

Think of getting commissions as a ladder.

At the bottom rung of the ladder are the leads you get. The next rung up are referrals, a better kind of lead. The rung after that is converting a lead to a listing or an offer. Then comes the sale, the escrow, the closing. And at the top of the ladder, the prize—the commission.

Your job is to climb the ladder. Do it successfully and you'll get the prize. But remember that you start climbing the ladder by lifting yourself up onto that first rung. Until you have leads, you really aren't on your way to commissions. Therefore, it behooves you to spend a large part of your time generating leads.

What, Exactly, Is a Lead?

Mark Twain (Samuel Clemens) said about the weather, "Everyone talks about it, but no one does anything about it!"

THE LADDER TO COMMISSIONS

_____/Commission
_____/Closing
_____/Escrow
_____/Converting to Listing or Offer
_____/Referral
_____/Lead

A lead is something like that—it's a tip, a pointer, a hint. Everyone involved in selling real estate knows that leads are important. But no one seems to be able to tell you, with clarity, how to easily go about getting them.

That's not because lead generation is a big secret. It's not. *Super-agents* employ techniques that generate huge numbers of leads for themselves. And many have written books and are giving seminars on their particular system.

I've read many of the books and attended some of the seminars, and what I've discovered is this: What works for one person usually does not work for another.

There are common threads running through what everyone does. But the amount of success generated is determined more by what works best for you than what others told you will work for them.

TRAP

Don't buy into *any* lead generation program, including this one. Read, think, try, and then find out what actually works best for you.

The Most Successful Agents Around

This is the story of a husband-and-wife team, Peter and Paula (called P2 by their associates). (That's not their real names or moniker, because I'm going to say some things about them that they might not appreciate.) They are immensely successful, having generated well over a million dollars in commissions between them for several years running. Currently they are out giving seminars charging over a thousand dollars per customer to hear how they generate leads.

I've watched them work, and I'll tell you how they do it ... for free.

P2 in the seminars will tell you about all of the various advertising and promotional gimmicks that they use. Indeed, they spend over $8,000 a month by their own admission on these various programs. (That's undoubtedly going to be well outside the limits of any new agent.)

They also point to the extended referral program that they use to get leads for those transferring into the area. They offer as much as a third of their commission to agents who send them solid leads on transferees.

And then they speak of their geographical farm (see next chapter) where they say they go door to door soliciting leads. Of course, in their case, they actually hire newcomers to do the leg work for them. (Don't be interested in doing this job; it doesn't pay well and usually doesn't lead anywhere.)

What they don't always mention, however, is what I call their "Aggressive Word-of-Mouth" plan. To my observation, this is how they get most of their million-dollar leads.

Peter and Paula sell the most expensive homes, typically a million dollars apiece and higher. They belong to an exclusive country club. It has a world-class golf course, and sometimes nationally televised golf tournaments are held there. It also has a dining room and bar where the financially elite in the community socialize. P2 are there most evenings. They mingle and they say just enough about their recent sales in the exclusive area to catch the interest of anyone thinking of buying or selling. They let it be known that they are the "hot team." I've heard them put down other agents that potential clients might mention. They point out that they've had more sales in the area than anyone else (which may or may not be true); they're the team that gets results. And, of course, they hand out their cards.

In essence, the country club is their office and their true lead generation source. It provides them with solid leads. I don't think P2 mention this much in their seminars. After all, why would they want the competition? Although it's doubtful anyone could easily compete.

After all, it's taken them over 20 years to build up this nice little lead generation program. They've worked hard to milk their farm for sale after sale. They are, indeed, well known there. It's unlikely any newcomer could waltz in and challenge them.

You're Unique

There are two important points to take away from the P2 example. The first is that whatever you do to generate leads, chances are if it's going to be successful it's also going to be unique. It's going to fit your personality, your pocketbook, your mode of operations.

Do listen to what others say, as I mentioned earlier, but take from that only what works for you. Don't buy wholeheartedly into any other system. Invent your own.

The Background Approach

There's another aspect to the P2 system that's worth noting. That's the money they spend each month on advertising. I like to call it creating a positive background. Here's what they do within the small geographical area where they work and live.

Advertising

- *Bus benches in the area.* P2 photos, names, phone numbers, and e-mail addresses are on all of them.

- *Shopping carts.* In three local grocery stores, every time you wheel a shopping cart, you are looking at P2 photos and their phone number and e-mail address.

- *Independent movie theaters in the area.* Before the previews start, there are P2 on the screen.

- *Local magazines.* Today, most cities have a city magazine. While in bigger cities, these are often full-blown (expensive) tomes, in smaller cities they are accessible. Open the small-town magazine in P2's area and you'll find their ad inside the front cover.

Now, if you're like me, it's unlikely you'll call up and then list (or even consider working with) an agent whose picture you saw on a bus bench. Indeed, you might feel negatively toward him or her.

But what if every time you went out shopping, attended the movie theater, passed by a bus bench, or picked up the local magazine there was their presence? Pretty soon you'd begin to remember the photo and the name, if not the phone number or e-mail address.

And then, what if you're at an exclusive social event and there they are? You'd recognize them already because of all the background publicity. Perhaps you'd be curious enough to go up to Peter or Paula, introduce yourself, and say how you've seen their pictures everywhere.

They are gracious, they smile, they make you feel like old-time friends. They point out that they are the team that everyone goes to when they want to buy or sell in the area. And you know what? You're ready to believe it!

The background advertising has done it for them. It's given them recognition and credibility. And ultimately, it has generated leads.

What Can You Do?

I'm not suggesting that, as you get started, you go out and spend eight grand a month on background advertising. After all, it really only works as background.

But I am suggesting that you think of lead generation in a more comprehensive manner than perhaps you've done before. In other words, put your picture on a bench, and it's wasted money.

However, knock on doors, send out mailers, do a newsletter, help with Little League and the American Youth Soccer Organization (AYSO), advertise listings with your name in large type in the local paper, and the effort all adds up, once you add in the personal touch.

TIP

In advertising it's common to speak of "touches" or contacts. How many times does it take for advertising to touch or contact a consumer before he or she takes notice and then takes action (presumably buying the product)? Some of the very best advertising needs only one contact. (Do you remember the Apple Macintosh advertisement with the female athlete throwing a hammer through a huge television screen, presumably with Big Blue on it, from the 1984 Super Bowl? It was only shown a couple of times, yet to this day people everywhere still remember it.) For most advertising, however, studies have been done that show touching the consumer might take as many as 30 to 40 contacts or more. That's seeing the same advertisement on television over 40 times before a consumer remembers the product and acts to buy it. (That's why the burger ads appear so often.)

In addition to a direct farming approach as outlined in detail in Chapter 6, you need to work on background advertising and publicity. It's not inexpensive. And it's not going to be done overnight. But, over time, it can lead to a huge lead generation system.

Open Houses: A Gateway to Leads

Here's a much underappreciated lead generator: the open house.

It's important to understand that there are two kinds of open houses. There are *broker's open houses*, where agents come by to see your property. And then there are *public open houses*, where prospective buyers and everyone else is invited to stop by. We're going to look at public open houses first. We'll consider broker's open houses next.

Countless studies have shown that people who come to public open houses rarely buy that house. Most visitors, in fact, are locals who just want to see what a neighbor's house looks like and what the asking price is. Others are just lookers hoping to find their dream house for a pittance.

Sellers love open houses, even though it rarely benefits them directly. Most experienced agents hate them because it ties up a valuable weekend.

For the new real estate agent who holds the open house, however, it can be a gold mine. Further, because experienced agents often are too busy to bother with holding open houses, those agents will sometimes be willing to delegate the work to a new agent, someone such as yourself. Thus, you can have all the opportunities that a public open house offers without actually having any listings of your own!

But what are the opportunities?

First of all, be sure you understand what we're talking about. Typically on a weekend day, sellers will leave for the afternoon and an agent will come in, leaving the doors unlocked and placing large signs in prominent positions in the yard and street that advertise, "Open House!" Really, anyone can come in.

If you're the agent—perhaps holding the Open house as a favor to a more experienced agent—it's your opportunity to strike up conversations with everyone who comes by.

Think of it as a magnificent opportunity. You aren't cold calling, you aren't even making the overture, the prospects are coming to you!

TIP

One agent I know specializes in just open houses. There's hardly a weekend that he doesn't produce at least one listing or purchase offer out of the "open".

Striking Up a Conversation (Gaining Rapport)

As part of your conversation with visitors, you can learn why they are coming to the open house. Here are some of the reasons in the order of their *priority for you*:

1. Anxious to immediately buy (or sell) in the neighborhood.
2. Looking to buy (or sell) within the next few months.
3. Trying to decide whether or not to buy (or sell).
4. Seeing what competitive houses look like (neighbors).
5. Just driving on a Saturday and thought it might be fun to stop by an open house.

Obviously, you're going to jump right on it if there's someone who's anxious to buy or sell immediately. But, even the lowest category, just driving by, should not be taken lightly. *Anyone* who comes to an open house has some interest in real estate, even if they don't express it at the moment—else why in the world would they really stop by?

If they themselves don't want to buy or sell in the near future, perhaps their neighbors do. Or their relatives. Or friends. Or business associates. Or someone they were talking to on a plane ride who happened to give them a business card on a completely unrelated matter.

TIP

I once made a sale to a passenger seated next to me on a short plane ride from Oakland to Los Angeles!

Everyone who comes by is at least a *warm* (if not *hot*) prospect, and should be treated as such based on the priority of how quickly they plan to act, and how much time you have available. (See Chapter 7 on converting leads.)

On the other hand, I've seen new agents totally mismanage an open house. Prospects have walked in and the agents simply smiled, said hello, asked them to sign in, and then went back to watching the ballgame on the seller's TV. What a waste!

TIP

When you meet someone at an open house, be sure you've done your homework. Be sure you know of at least five other similar nearby listed houses that are for sale. If the lookers decide they don't like the open house, which is likely, be prepared to tell them about just the other right home for them. Arrange to take them out. If you have someone covering for you, take the lookers out to the other house right then—don't wait. You could get an immediate sale.

NOTE

Never close up and leave an open house. You're doing a disservice to the listing agent and the seller. Prearrange for another beginning agent to share the open house with you, so you can cover for each other if an opportunity comes up to take a potential buyer elsewhere.

TRAP

Many agents pooh-pooh the leads derived from an open house. They use terms such as "lookers" and "dreamers." Probably most do fit this category. But, there are over 70 million home owners in this country, and the average duration of home ownership (time between buying and selling) is under nine years. If you're in it for the long haul, chances are that most of those who stop by will buy or sell within the next nine years. You're talking to potential clients no matter how uninterested they may seem at the time.

Broker's Open

A broker's open house, although it too is called an open house, is something quite different from the seller's open.

If you've got a listing, a broker's open is an excellent way to generate a sale and a listing commission for yourself. When you hold a broker's open, you're using the system. You're tapping into the network of agents in your area, some of whom may actually be working with buyers who could be interested in the very home that you're showing. (When you're looking for a buyer, it's also a good way to quickly learn about listed property in your area.)

TIP

Offer food, and they will come. Want to attract a lot of agents to your broker's open? Then let everyone know you're providing sandwiches, light drinks, snacks, and so on. Hold your broker's open in the early afternoon (around lunchtime) and you should have a packed house. It can be expensive, but I've seen it get results.

While it's true that buyers rarely purchase the open house they visit, it's just as true that agents who come by often are looking for homes such as this listing for their clients. Buyer's open frequently result in offers and then sales.

On the other hand, know which side of the bread the butter is on. It's to no advantage to you to help out another agent on a broker's open unless it's your own listing, or the listing agent is cutting you in for a piece of the commission. Don't expect to generate leads on a broker's open house. Remember, it's *for agents!*

Does Cold Calling Really Work?

At some time in your career, your broker is probably going to direct you to get out there and do some cold calling. Typically, this means simply going down the phone book (or reverse phone book) and calling up people in a neighborhood, introducing yourself, and ultimately asking if they are going to be selling their house or know of anyone else who wants to sell or buy.

The reason you'll be asked to do this is threefold:

- *It keeps you busy.* Many new agents waste a lot of their time moping around the office looking for something to do. This gets you on the phone and out of your broker-manager's hair.

- *It holds out the promise of finding a prospect.* After all, someone you touch on the phone might just be ready to sell ... and you can be the first to connect up with them.

- *It teaches you to sink or swim.* Many agents who find this distasteful, undignified, and very difficult, soon wash out. Presumably, those who succeed at it soon become great successes in real estate.

Over the years, I've talked to many real estate agents about cold calling. Usually they defend the process, saying that, yes, once they did get a good lead from a cold call. But, when asked if they do it now, invariably they say, "No, I really don't have time." Most of the super-agents I've spoken with refuse to *ever* do any cold calling. Rather, if they do make blind calls to prospects, it's what might be termed "warm" calling. They use lists derived from people who have previously called their office or otherwise made contact with them, first.

My suggestion is that you'll save yourself a lot of time and headaches by simply saying, "No," when your broker-manager-trainer directs you to cold call. Yes, you could develop a lead or two. But the months of effort involved, to my mind, are simply not worth the results. You could do far better at other approaches suggested by this book.

TRAP

If you decide to call, be sure you first check with the *DO NOT CALL* list in your area. These are the phone numbers of people who have opted out from having unsolicited calls and have registered with the Federal Trade Commission at 1-888-382-1222. If you call some-one on the list and they make a record of your call, you and your broker could be subject to severe fines.

Unusual Places to Find Leads

Remember, what works for one person will not necessarily work for another. Here are two unusual lead generation programs that I've seen make their agents rich. Can you use all or part of either of them?

The Rental Lead Generation Service

Rentals are always a part of real estate. However, almost no agent I know wants to bother with them. After all, they take a lot of time, often you have to spend hours showing a house, and in the end, you're lucky if you get one or at most two months' rent as a commission, which you then have to split with your broker! Where's the profit in it?

Let's take the story of Sylvia. She managed a drive-through restaurant, but wanted to do something bigger and better in life. So, she got her license and went into real estate.

It was very hard for Sylvia to get started in the business. Listings were tough to come by, and the buyers she found had champagne tastes and beer budgets. Months went by without any commissions.

Finally, Sylvia's broker took pity on her. She told her that every real estate office likes to handle rentals. That way, when a client wants to move out of the area and keep the house, the agency can rent it for him or her. Eventually, a listing can come out of it. She asked Sylvia to handle the office's rentals.

"What do I have to lose?" Sylvia asked herself.

So she handled the few rentals that the other agents fell into. Then she read up on property management, took a course on the subject, and began to quietly advertise as a property manager.

Soon she had her own clients, for whom she rented homes and in one case a six-plex. She kept her business small—single-family and a few multifamily buildings. She didn't go into property managing condominiums or developments, which she felt were beyond her abilities.

She did well. And within a year, she found that she was getting a steady flow of leads from her rental owners. Invariably, they wanted to sell and buy other properties. Also, she was able to convert some of her tenants to buyers. So, soon she had a long list of "captive" buyers, loyal to her because of her rental relationship to them.

Her business grew until eventually she got her own broker's license, and opened her own small office. It wasn't prominently placed on any street; rather it was in the back of a strip mall. But she didn't care. It was perfect for tenants to come to both when they wanted to rent and when they became buyers. Also she could work out of it very well when it came to finding investment properties and selling them for owners. Best of all, the rent was cheap keeping her overhead down.

The key, of course, were the leads. Sylvia turned a loser into a winner. She took what no one else wanted, and she made a successful lead generation program out of it.

Can you take some of this story, apply it to yourself, and use it to generate your own leads?

The Mobile Home Agent

Here's another true story.

Very few in real estate care about or want to bother with mobile home sales. And for good reason.

Difficulties with Mobile Home Sales:

- *Low commissions.* The homes are often priced at a fourth or less of what conventional homes sell for, hence much lower commissions.

- *Hard to move.* While the general housing market may be booming, it may take 3 to 6 months to find a buyer for a mobile home.

- *The hassles.* There are frequently more government rules and regulations regarding the sale of mobile homes (considered part vehicle/part real property) in many states than apply to conventional homes.

In some areas, those who list mobile homes are considered losers, those who simply can't get any other listings. And often these listings simply go onto the multiple listing service and languish there.

George, however, who was new to real estate, noticed that because few agents bothered with mobile homes, it was a wide-open field. There was little competition, and there were lots of sellers clamoring for action. Where others saw difficulty, he saw opportunity.

So, he began to learn everything about mobile homes. He located all the parks in his area and proceeded to canvass them going door-to-door.

He quickly learned that the turnover rate was high in those older parks that were for occupants aged "55 and older." Most had been built 20 to 30 years earlier and now the residents were moving to retirement homes, to convalescent hospitals, or the homes were being sold by heirs after their owners passed away. These he decided to farm.

Since there was little competition, his signs were soon all over the place. And buyers seeing them tended to come to him first. The leads were plentiful.

Although it took a few years, he eventually established himself as the dominant broker in the mobile home park area. As a result he had many round-trips (double-pops, double-bubbles, or whatever the term in your area is for being both the listing and selling agent).

Further, because the prices weren't high, the sellers were willing to pay a 10 percent commission. When he got all of it, it often amounted to more than he would have gotten on a split on a conventional home.

Eventually George got a better deal with his broker than just splitting commissions. He began to pay for his desk space and other expenses (see Chapter 5). He handled all of his expenses and simply paid a flat fee to operate out of the broker's office. He liked the "cover" the office gave him and didn't want to move on to operating his own office. It all worked, of course, because of the lead generation program he developed with mobile homes, a "farm" that he controlled.

Do you disdain working the mobile home market? Have you tried it? Can you take some of George's lessons and apply them to yourself?

Look for the Unwanted

George's and Sylvia's lead generation success can be attributed in large part to their creativity and their open eyes. They each found a pile of lemons and made lemonade. They took an area where other agents didn't want to tread and made it their own.

TIP

Go where no one else wants to go to find your path to success.

Should you go into the rental business? Or the mobile home sales business? Will they generate leads for you?

Maybe. Or, maybe it's not for you, and some other avenue will present itself.

Try to think "outside the box." If you've having trouble generating leads, look for avenues in your area where others don't want to go. Turn them around. Be creative.

Remember, everyone's success is unique. Find a way to make yours.

Developing the Lifetime Customer

The best leads, of course, are the ones who come back time after time. They are the buyers who are totally loyal to you. If they are homeowners, they were probably immensely pleased with the service you first gave them and are now repeating. As long as you maintain your high-level service, you'll continue to get these people as clients.

An even better lead can be the investor in real estate. Typically these people buy homes or small multifamily dwellings. The advantage here is they usually make far more purchases and sales than the occupant owner described above. While an occupant owner may purchase and sell a home once every 7 to 9 years, an investor may do so every year or two, sometimes more often. If this person buys and sells exclusively through you, he or she becomes your "franchise."

The difficulty, of course, is in keeping the franchise. Investors tend to shop around for agents. You have to ask yourself, why should an investor keep coming back to you?

Yes, of course, service is important. But to investors, even more important is making a profit.

There are two ways to turn an investor into a permanent franchise. The first is to continuously keep coming up with deals that nobody else can find. While you would hope to be able to do this, it's doubtful you can succeed over time.

The second way is to cut the investor a special price. Perhaps you'll reduce the commission on every sale, providing the investor buys exclusively through you. Or buys at least two properties a year through you.

Most agents abhor cutting their commission, their life blood, so to speak. But that's only when talking about a single sale. What if we're talking about a dozen sales over a few years? Any smart agent should be happy to more than make up in volume what is lost in a commission reduction.

The other avenue is to go partners with the investor. Many agents will "invest" part or all of their commission in the investor's property for a share of the profits down the road. If prices are appreciating and you can handle the deferral of a cash commission to an even bigger payday later on, it's something to seriously consider.

Record Your Leads

You've got to know what works for you.

It's important to write down every lead and where it comes from. While this effort may take a few moments over time, it will help you immensely to organize yourself so that you know where your most promising sources are.

TRAP

Don't rely on your memory! While sources may seem perfectly clear today, a month from now they may all blend together, and six months from now you may not have a clue. Take the time to write them down!

The following are some sources that you may find are very productive. Note, the order of importance may be different for each agent.

Typical Sources of Leads, in Order of Importance
1. Close friends
2. Relatives
3. Open houses
4. Social organizations
5. Service clubs
6. Internet
7. Geographical farming (Going door to door)
8. Advertising
9. Floor time
10. Working FSBOs
11. Working expired listings

When you get a lead, create a category such as one of those above, then put a check after it to indicate that's where the lead came from. (You should put the name, date, address, and a brief description of the lead elsewhere; see Chapter 10 for computer programs to help you organize your leads.)

After six months or a year, you can go back and see where your most productive area is. For example, for you it may be the Internet. Perhaps you have a "Wow!" site that's driving people right to your door. If that's the case, put the Internet in the number one spot and devote most of your energies there.

Focusing on that one special area could mean you'll cut back on advertising, or open houses, or whatever is not productive.

TRAP

I have seen elaborate schemes created to determine where your best source of leads comes from. These include converging circles to graphically portray lead sourcing. Or defining in detail the number of times you "touch" others with a phone call, personal appearance, or promotion. Or even creating a vast database in a PDA. Just keep in mind that we're not talking brain surgery here. To my way of thinking, you want to avoid wheel spinning. Yes, you need to know the information. But, you don't need to take time away from business to create an elaborate system to let you know. Keep it simple, keep it quick, keep it accurate. If you devote only a few minutes a day to sourcing your leads, that's all you need.

Every agent instinctively knows that he or she needs leads to succeed. Leads are the bread and butter of real estate agents. As such, leads *lead*.

Find a lead generation program that works for you and stick with it. Over time, it will make you more successful than you can imagine.

6
What Your Broker Never Told You About Farming

If you've ever taken a course that talks about how to sell real estate, the word *farming* has surely come up. Many brokers consider it the basic fare of the agent: they teach that you can't succeed without your real estate farm. It's what provides you with leads and listings.

While there's a lot of truth to that, unfortunately most agents are taught the wrong concept about what a farm really is. They think of a farm as something physical: houses, a tract, a neighborhood, a geographical area.

While it can certainly involve all of those things, it's important to keep focused on the donut and not the hole. Houses don't give you listings; people give them to you. Thus, a farm is best described as an association of people. While the most common association is, in fact, in a neighborhood, it doesn't necessarily have to be. You can farm the people whom you meet and solicit at a book club, on a Little League team, at a church outing, or as we'll shortly see, in some other rather unlikely places.

What Is "Farming a Neighborhood?"

The concept was first introduced in the 1950s by early franchise companies as a way of helping new salespeople get started in the business.

The broker would tell a salesperson that the office was dividing up the local neighborhoods. "The Oakwood Hills tract is now your farm. Go out there and knock on doors. Cold call the residents. Get to know the area and let the people get to know you. When they want to sell, they'll call you back and you'll get listings."

TIP

Farming people can be a highly effective tool for getting listings and referrals. When handled properly, it can provide a lifelong and highly successful career for an agent.

Did this type of "canvassing" work?

Certainly. The harder the agent "worked" the farm (getting to know the residents), the more leads, referrals, and listings came out of it. Agents quickly and mistakenly came to regard geographical farming as the *only* key to success in real estate.

Today, most brokers still tell their salespeople essentially the same thing, "Go out there and farm!" Many salespeople, though not most, work hard at their farming, at least at first. They walk the neighborhood and knock door to door, make phone calls, send mailings, contact people by e-mail, and do everything they can to become known as "the agent to call when you want to list your home."

Only there's a big problem. While one broker and his or her salespeople can easily divide up a city and farm neighborhoods, today there are many other realty offices around. We don't live and work in a vacuum.

TRAP

There are over a million real estate agents in the country competing with one another. That number represents at least a 30 percent increase after the most recent property boom at the turn of the century.

If there are two offices around, then chances there are two or maybe even three salespeople are farming the same neighborhood. If a dozen offices are nearby, then dozens of agents may be farming the same area.

Think of the confusion if a dozen different agricultural farmers tried to farm the same plot of land. Chances are, nothing would grow.

Today, with the proliferation of offices and the large number of agents (more than a million nationwide at last count and still growing), there isn't a neighborhood in virtually any city in the country that isn't being farmed. Thus, in order to succeed at farming, you need to work harder and harder. And dominance on the farm is ever more difficult to achieve.

TIP

Most people have only one person in each profession that they "call their own"—their own doctor, their own dentist, their own attorney, and their own real estate agent. Unless you "belong" to them, you won't get called when they need to list or buy. The whole goal of successful farming is to be that chosen one.

How to Get Leads from a Fertile Geographical Farm

In a few paragraphs we're going to move on to farming people, directly, *without* regard to neighborhood. But for now, consider the traditional method of farming. How can you choose the best geographical area to farm? Here are six questions you need to answer.

Is It the Right Size?

Neighborhoods can be too small or too large for efficient farming. If there are only 50 homes, then you simply don't have enough properties changing hands to eke out a living for you. If 20 percent are sold each year (a very high number), that's only 10 homes and 10 commissions, assuming you get all the listing (very unlikely). Unless the houses are extremely expensive, there simply isn't enough money involved to make working the *small* farm worthwhile.

On the other hand, *if* the houses are expensive, it's a different story.

Notice that as the homes get more expensive, the same number of sales yields a far higher potential income for the agent.

Table 6.1 Average-Priced Small Farm versus
Expensive-Priced Small Farm

Inexpensive Homes	
Average home price	$250,000
Average commission of 6%	15,000
Total sales commissions available (? 10)	150,000
Expensive Homes	
Average home price	$1,000,000
Average commission of 6%	60,000
Total sales commissions available (? 10)	600,000

TIP

One of the themes of this book is to concentrate on working more expensive homes. It's working smarter, not harder.

Many old timers will tell you the ideal neighborhood is 300 to 400 homes. That's sufficiently large enough to provide plenty of sales. Yet it's not so large as to overcome your ability to service the area.

Unfortunately, when inventories are low and with today's competition, 300 to 400 homes may simply not be enough. Today, a farm of closer to a thousand homes (often comprising several neighborhoods, although in a proximate geographical area) is necessary. Fortunately, with the advent of computers, the Internet, fax machines, and cell phones, it is possible to service (with hard work) such a large number of homes.

Does It Have a Good Rate of Turnover?

You can easily find out the rate of turnover by checking sales in the area through the MLS. The fact is that some neighborhoods have a very high turnover rate. Often these are fairly new areas with owners who have frequent job changes. On the other hand, areas that are more established with more mature owners tend to have lower turnover rates.

Ideally you'd want a neighborhood where 25 percent of the homes sold each year. That's a very high rate, and also very difficult to find. A more likely good turnover rate is 15 percent a year. However, even at that rate, if there are 1,000 homes in the farm, that's 150 houses. If you dominate the farm and get most of those listings, and if the homes are fairly expensive, you can make a very nice living out of it.

TOTAL COMMISSION AVAILABLE ON A LARGE, FAIRLY EXPENSIVE TRACT

Average home price	$ 500,000
Average commission at 6%	30,000
Total sales commissions available (? 150)	$4,500,000

Is It Close to Where You Work and Live?

If possible, try to live within your farm. Doing so has decided advantages. When you speak to an owner of a home in the farm, you can say, "I'm your neighbor—I just live down the street (or one block over or whatever)."

As soon as you say this, you become a "we" instead of a "they." Even if the homeowner has never laid eyes on you before, he or she knows you face the same neighborhood issues (crime, noise, new construction, remodeling, and so on). You're more likely to be *simpatico* with them. No, you're not an instant friend. But, you are an instant neighbor. And people are far more likely to listen to—and eventually list with—a neighbor than an "outsider."

There are other good reasons for living within, or at least close to, your farm. For one thing, it's simply easier to get there. Whether you're farming, making a listing presentation, showing a home, or working an escrow, it's only a hop, step, and a jump for you to get to the subject property. You can service the seller, and the buyer, so much better.

Furthermore, when you get a call and you need to quickly get down there to make a listing presentation, you can do it in minutes, instead of hours. You can beat out the competition with your speed, because of your access.

Finally, because you live there, you're likely to more intimately know the houses—their advantages and little problems. When someone complains about the poor location of the fireplace in the living room, you can nod understandingly, because your home has a similar problem. You can tell them that the builder did it to save money... and then go on to explain how you solved that particular architectural drawback by a special arrangement of the furniture. It's something only a fellow homeowner might know.

It should go without saying that you should learn everything you can about your farm houses: size, shape, square footage, floor plans, décor, price, and so on. But actually living there tends to make you far more credible—and knowledgeable.

Is the Price Range of the Homes Adequate?

As we've seen, the more expensive the property, the bigger the commission and the bigger your income.

TIP

The amount of work involved in selling an expensive house probably is going to be more than that for an inexpensive house—but not that much more!

This is not to say that you should ever turn down a listing that you can properly service and sell regardless of the price of the property. If someone comes to you and says, "Please list my $125,000 house," and you know it will sell for that price, you'd be a foolish agent to turn the listing down.

On the other hand, if your farm is made up of mainly of $125,000 houses, then that's the price range almost all of your leads and referrals are going to be. It's what you'll get because it's what you're aiming for.

On the other hand, if you aim higher, say for a farm where the average price is $400,000 or more, then that's the average-priced listing you're likely to get. Remember, you'll work just as hard on a farm where the houses average $125,000 as you will where they average $400,000 or more.

TRAP

There's an old expression in agricultural farming that goes, "It's not worth a hill of beans!" The meaning behind it is that beans are such a poor crop, that they're almost not worth farming. Compare that to a rich crop, such as strawberries, and you'll often have the difference between a successful agricultural farmer … and a failure. Plant strawberries, not beans.

Is the Competition Vulnerable?

It's not a question of whether or not there will be competitors. There will be. The only question is, does one of them dominate the area you are considering farming? Or is it open for grabs?

How do you know? There are several ways to tell.

Know Your Competition

- *Sales.* Is there one agent who seems to have most (more than half) of the sales in the area? You can quickly check this out on the MLS. If there's an agent who has 75 percent of the sales in an area, that's domination! Even 50 percent indicates an agent who is successfully controlling the action. It's usually far easier to pick a farm that doesn't have a dominant agent than to challenge such an agent for control.

TIP

Look at both the listing and selling side. Sometimes an agent who dominates a farm will lose a listing to another agent (a relative or special friend of the seller), only to come in and provide the buyer.

- *Signs.* Drive the streets. If most of the For Sale signs in the farm are for one agent, that person is dominating the area. On the other hand, if the signs are for many different offices and agents, it's an indication that the area is vulnerable. Here you'll have a better chance to establish yourself.

- *Comments.* Even after you've tentatively decided on an area, be sure you walk it and talk to some of the neighbors. Ask them if there's a particular agent who they might use if they list. (People are surprisingly open about this question, though few agents ever ask it.) If one name keeps cropping up again and again, you know you've got fierce competition.

- *Events.* These days many neighborhoods have events on a regular basis. There are picnics, Christmas parties, soccer, Little League teams in local parks, and so on. Find out who organizes these and learn if there's a particular person, often a real estate agent, who always does the barbecuing, or who dresses up like a clown for the kids, or who provides the sodas, or whatever. You get the idea. Chances are that everyone knows and loves this agent and he or she is going to get the listings, not you.

If the competition is vulnerable (doesn't control the listings and sales in the area), it's an invitation for you to move in. If you're aggressive and follow the steps outlined later in this chapter, you should do well.

On the other hand, if there is an agent who dominates the farm, move on. There are plenty of other farms and, as noted, it will be far easier to establish yourself in a farm where the other agents are vulnerable than to fight an agent who already has control. Remember, most people only think of *one* agent as "theirs." If someone else already holds that spot, you'll find it difficult to supplant him or her.

What Are the Tools You Need for Farming?

We've already discussed many of them. They include walking the neighborhood and calling on owners, making phone calls, sending promotions through the mail, using the Internet, participating in neighborhood events, and more. Check the end of this chapter for a list of things you can do to be a more effective farmer.

Why Geographical Farming Fails

Most, that's more than half, of all agents who start out with high hopes and good intentions, fail miserably at farming a neighborhood. Most last less than a year. Many are gone after two or three months.

With a failure rate that high, either farming must be incredibly difficult or most agents are doing something wrong.

Since farming is straightforward, with very few secrets, then my conclusion is that most agents are doing something wrong. Here are the four big reasons that most agents fail at farming.

Four Big Reasons for Geographical Farming Failures

Bad Choice of Where to Farm.?   Reread the section above on selecting a farm. Then ask yourself:

- *Is it big enough?* Chances are, your farm is too small to be successful. Expand your area or consider a people farm, which is explained below.

- *Do you live nearby?* Many agents choose their farm area because of price range, turnover rates, and lack of competition and figure it doesn't really matter if they live in it or nearby. But it does. You could be overworking and underproducing because you live too far from your farm.

TRAP

Canvassing can be dangerous. The most common method of farming a geographical area is to walk the neighborhood and knock on doors. You introduce yourself to those who are home and leave a card or pamphlet for those that aren't. What could be safer? However, recently in a prestigious neighborhood of Los Angeles, a young agent in his late twenties was shot and seriously wounded when he knocked on a door. He didn't even talk to anyone inside. He simply left his card, turned to leave, and the resident, who had apparently come around the house, shot him in the abdomen with a shotgun. It was a drug house and the real estate agent had been mistaken for an undercover policeman. No, it's not a common occurrence. In fact, it's extremely uncommon. But it could happen ... and has happened.

- *Is there enough turnover?* This is among the first things you should check. If the neighborhood has a low turnover rate (5 percent or less sales in a year), bail out. It just isn't fertile enough to make it successful.

- *Is the competition too fierce?* Remember, it's far harder to dislodge an established agent who dominates a farm, than to move into one where the competition is vulnerable.

- *Is the price range too low?* If the houses aren't pricy enough, you'll be working yourself ragged, getting lots of commissions, making lots of sales ... and still not move into the area of a super-agent.

You Didn't Stick with It Long Enough? Everyone likes to see success, and quickly. Begin working hard on a farm and if, after a month or two, you don't have a single listing, I guarantee you're going to get discouraged. If that's the case, then reexamine the one above and the two below. If you're okay there, then give it longer. Remember, you're building a career here. And that doesn't happen in weeks or even months. It could take years. It's the agent who has the staying power who eventually becomes the big winner, the super-agent.

You Didn't Work Hard Enough?   When you first start out farming, you need to spend every day working on your farm. That can mean setting aside four to six hours for farming. And those must be productive hours. See the section at the end of this chapter on farming tools and also Chapter 4 on managing your time. Also, keep in mind that it's possible to *think* you're working hard when actually you're just spinning your wheels. It won't hurt to sit down with a friend (preferably another, more experienced agent—a mentor, if possible) and explain what you're doing. See what the other person says. Sometimes an honest outside opinion is all it takes to turn things around.

You Spoke to the Wrong People?   I've seen this happen. An agent spends time, money, and effort walking the neighborhood, making calls, sending out promotions, all of which go to tenants and never find their way to owners. (Tenants most likely will simply throw away your card and mailings.) Make the effort to find out who owns the property. You can get the records at the county recorder's office or sometimes from old MLS files. Some neighborhoods have as many as 25 percent or more tenants. If that's the case, then you could have been wasting 25 percent of your efforts. Make sure you know whom you're talking to, and that it's the owner of the property.

TIP

A nonoccupant owner (landlord) is just as good a farming prospect as an owner who lives in the property. After all, they will eventually want to sell and list, too. Be sure to find out the owner's address and direct your promotions to him or her.

What Is "Farming" People?

This leads us to a different kind of farming, for people. Let's consider Terri:

Terri was new to the business, but she was eager to learn and enthusiastic. After getting a few listings (and sales) from all the friends and relatives (and their friends and associates) she had, she realized, to expand her horizon. So, she attended a few seminars and read a few books, all of which promised her that the key to becoming hugely successful was to become a "farmer." So she set up the boundaries of a geographic farm in her area and set to work with a vengeance:

- She sent out letters of introduction
- She walked the neighborhood with another agent (for security), introducing herself and passing out brochures and her business card.
- She bought professional business reports and sent them to those living within her farm on a regular basis.
- She made phone calls and asked if people had received her reports.
- She sent out cards that notified people when one of their neighbors sold a home.
- She established a "Notes from Terri" newsletter and filled it with recipes, a calendar of coming events in the community, and inspirational quotes from famous people, which she sent out to those in her farm every other month.

All of these techniques over time produced some leads. And she converted some of these to listings and eventually to sales.

Of course, the big problem was that her farm wasn't hers alone. Nearly a dozen other agents were farming the same territory at roughly the same time. Competition is hot in today's real estate, and agents fight bitterly over farm areas.

Thus, in order to keep her volume up, she had to work harder and harder to expand her farm. She found she was putting in 10 and 12-hour days and rarely taking a full day off. (She would try to take days off, but she was always on call and, inevitably, someone would call her during her intended time off.)

Terri worked hard at it for one and a half years. During that time she made many sales. However, she was run ragged. Her income one year topped $60,000. However, she never achieved the status of a *super-agent*. Terri was working harder, but not necessarily smarter. Eventually, she just couldn't stand it anymore and left real estate.

Terri took some course work and became a state licensed cosmetologist. She worked in an upscale beauty salon. Terri was ever open for opportunities and soon realized that she was doing the hair of mostly women, but some men, who lived in a very upscale area. They constantly talked with her and confided in her about their concerns and problems. While mostly these involved their kids and marital issues (including divorce and infidelity), they sometimes also involved discussions about money and specifically about buying and selling real estate.

With her experience (Terri had "parked" her license with a friendly broker), Terri was a champ at talking about real estate, and more and more of her clients sought out her opinions and advice. Many said she should go back into the business. One day, out of the blue, a client offered a listing on her multimillion-dollar house. Terri, who had still had her real estate license active, accepted. Within three days she had sold the house to another client who, while getting her hair dyed, said she was looking for just such a residence.

Terri got a double pop, both selling and listing commission, and after splitting with her broker, walked away with over $40,000.

Terri, as W.C. Fields used to say, "knew which side of the bread the butter was on."

She opened a small office nearby and set about "farming" her beauty salon clients in earnest. When they learned she was actively selling real estate (in addition to doing their hair) and had actually sold a multimillion-dollar home, some jumped on board.

To this day Terri does a *super-agent* business and specializes in expensive properties, and on many of which she handles both sides of the deal. Now she's a broker, but she doesn't belong to a franchise, although she joined the local real estate board and the MLS. Her office is a little hole in the wall, but that's not where she really does her business. That she does in the beauty salon, where she farms the people whose hair she works on. One thing she knows for certain— she'll never quit her day job. It's a gold mine!

TIP

You can't really farm houses; they're simply wood, bricks, mortar, and nails. You can only farm people. It's one of the most important concepts you can learn.

How to Find Your People Farm

A people farm can be anywhere. One agent I know farms at his Masonic Lodge. I understand the order frowns on such activities, so he simply lets everyone know his profession is in real estate and that he's damn good at it. He still gets his share of the business.

TRAP

Beware of farming the traditional service clubs such as the Lion's or Rotary. Chances are that there may already be many other members doing the same thing.

Another agent teaches a course in real estate at a nearby college on a part-time basis. While he's teaching his students the principles of real estate investing, he demonstrates his prowess and success in the field. He has not only gotten listings and referrals from them, but he has also gone into several joint ventures with students that proved highly profitable.

Yet another agent I know works the tennis courts. He belongs to a local tennis club and is constantly looking for games with newcomers. After the game, there's often a wind-down period over a drink (usually nonalcoholic), and the subject of professions comes up. He isn't hesitant to tell what a great real estate agent he is, how many properties he's sold, and he winds up telling the other person to check it out. When he hand them his card, he also hands them a short list of recent sales. "Call them. Ask them if they were satisfied."

The other player often protests he's not selling his house. But my tennis friend says, "It doesn't matter. When you do, you'll remember me." And they frequently do.

TRAP

Remember, the single biggest mistake you can make is to think of a farm as strictly an area of land. It's not. It's people. And if you once understand you're farming people, not houses, your farm is limited only by your imagination.

The Essential Farm Tools

Here are some lists of items that you can use to promote yourself to your farm. You've probably heard of many; some will be too expensive to use, but others can be obtained at minimal expense and effort.

Remember, however, that none of these alone will likely get you a listing or a sale. Rather, when used consistently as part of a "background" and when coupled with personal contacts, they can be highly effective in producing solid leads.

Promotional Items to Be Sent to People in Your Farm

- Doorhangers that you can personally distribute to tell of Just Sold listings.
- Cards that tell of Just Listed homes in the area.
- Informational flyers that give local market statistics (with your name and photo prominently placed, of course).
- Get-acquainted cards, notes, and flyers, including recipes, calendars, inspirational comments, gardening tips, pool care tips, local real estate investment news, house maintenance tips, and other useful information.
- Newsletters put out on a monthly basis that give your views of the market. (You can enhance your views by seeing what others are putting out nationally on a variety of Web sites including my own, www.robertirwin.com.)
- Your name, logo, and contact information on a business card, refrigerator magnet, or other convenient-to-keep media.
- Digital photos that can be sent to your prospects via e-mail.
- Videos of yourself showing property that you can use to help convince a seller to list.
- Thank-you cards for referrals or for other services performed by a prospect.

TRAP

The above-mentioned items are sometimes referred to as "throwaways." Yes, they do frequently get thrown away, but many also get saved. Don't get into the habit of thinking of them as throwaways, or else you'll not want to spend money on them and won't use them wisely. Think of them as "lead generators."

All of the above items are expensive because they are not the sort of thing you buy and send once. Rather, they are meant to be repeat items, sent out monthly, quarterly, or annually to a large number of people. Thus, you'll need a budget for them.

When you're first starting out, however, money is usually very tight. So my suggestion is that you get only the essentials, which include business cards and stationery. Then, as you can afford to (as the commission checks roll in), you set up a budget to handle these items. Generally speaking, promotional costs shouldn't exceed 4 or 5 percent of your income.

Remember, none of the above alone will likely get you a listing or a sale. But, used in combination (especially with personal contact) with one another, they form a positive background that will enhance your success.

Advertising

We all know that advertising pays (else "free" television and radio, newspapers, magazines, and so on simply wouldn't be around). Unfortunately, advertising also costs a lot.

The amount you spend on advertising, as with promotional items, should be limited by the amount of income you have. When you're first starting out, don't even dream of advertising. (Your broker should handle basic listing advertising for you.) However, as your success grows, then add in advertising as much as possible.

Advertising in general is far more expensive than promotional items. However, it should never exceed 10 percent of your income and is better if kept below 7 percent.

TIP

Think of advertising as something that helps grow your business bigger, not of something that helps you get off the ground.

Advertising Possibilities	Cost	Effectiveness
Local theaters ads	Minimal	Average
Major newspapers	High	High
Local magazines	Average	Minimal
Local billboards	High	Minimal
Local bus benches	Average	Minimal
Commercial television	High	Minimal
Community television	Minimal	Average
Yellow Pages of phone book	Very High	Average
Grocery store buggies	Average	Average
E-mail	Minimal	Minimal
Property signs	Minimal	High
Car/Van Signs	Average	Minimal
Sponsorship (soccer, Little League, charities, etc.)	Minimal	High

7

Converting Leads and Referrals to Listings

You get a call from a friend of a friend, a business associate or someone in your farm (see the last chapter on farming). He is thinking of listing his property and he has heard you're in real estate. Do you have time to come over and tell him how much his home is really worth?

TIP

Leads seldom call up and say, "Come get a listing." The vast majority are standoffish. They're probably not sold on you, yet. (They may be planning on calling others as well.) They just want a pricing opinion, or some direction on what they should do to make their home ready for sale, or just a chance to talk more with you. Now it's up to you to convert this lead to a solid listing. How well you can do this may very well determine your future in real estate.

So, you're off to make a presentation. The question arises, all else being equal, why should people select you as "their agent" and list with you? What makes you "their agent," the one person with whom they'll trust their future fortunes?

The following are three good reasons that people will list (as well as make an offer, if they're buyers) with you.

Reason Number 1 for Selecting You: People Love or at Least Like You

The number one reason people select an agent is because they like or even love you.

It's the sort of thing that politicians run up against all the time. One candidate is far smarter than the other, better dressed, seems to be more in tune with the issues, even has more money to spend on campaigning. But that candidate loses because his or her opponent is more loved by the voters. Being loved means that people trust you to do right by them. They'll come to you over someone else every time.

Being loved is an amorphous, nebulous, vague feeling that is almost impossible to pin down. Few, however, would argue that it doesn't exist. And if people love you, they'll do almost anything for you, including signing a listing agreement.

Of course, we can't all be loved. If you can't be loved, then you must at least be liked. People will also list with and buy property through someone whom they like.

On the other hand, if you produce a negative response, you're in trouble. I can't imagine doing business with anyone whom I dislike. It almost doesn't make any difference what that person is offering; if I don't care for that individual, I won't have anything to do with him or her. I suspect that most people feel the same way.

So, how do you become that endearing, lovable, or at least likable, person?

Some people are just naturally that way. If you're the sort who everyone loves to be around, then good for you. (By the way, you're definitely in the minority!)

On the other hand, if you're the kind of person who doesn't have a lot of charisma, establishing likability is going to be trickier. If you're the sort who simply gets lost in a crowd or who is forgettable (it's a sure clue if your mother-in-law can't remember your name), then you have a lot of work to do.

The good news is that it is possible to learn how to become more likable. And if you're really successful at it, even become lovable.

I have found four characteristics (all learnable, by the way) that are almost always present in such a person.

Characteristics That Make an Agent Likable and/or Lovable

You Have Integrity (You're Always Being Honest). No one likes a dishonest person. He or she can't be trusted. Of course, being honest is easy when it doesn't count, when there isn't any money on the line. People have integrity when they tell the truth, even though it might hurt them financially. An example is when you risk losing a listing by telling sellers what their home is really worth, not the fantasy price they have imagined. Another example is when you stop by a home in your neighborhood and openly tell the owner that you're farming and hope she'll eventually list with you. A person who has integrity won't lie and will seldom even exaggerate.

TIP

An important part of having integrity is to never run down your competitors. If a homeowner or a client asks about them, you can simply say you hold them in highest regard. If you don't, just say nothing.

Why not run down your competitors when there might be all sorts of nasty things you say about them?

There are three good reasons.

- *When you run someone else down, it makes you look small and, to a certain extent, despicable.* It doesn't matter if your views happen to be true. (Of course, if the competitor's license was just revoked, you might want to mention that.)

- *It can get back to the other person.* You can't control information once it's out of your mouth. You don't know who will repeat it. And you can be sure that if the competitor hears about it, you'll have made an enemy, which you certainly don't need, especially when you're just starting out. And if others hear about it, they'll forever think of you as unprofessional.

- *If you pass rumors about another agent, your clients may wonder if you'll later say something bad about them.* So, they may trust you just a little bit less. At this juncture, you want all the trust you can get.

You're Always on the Client's Side. Many agents get frustrated when sellers and buyers do stupid things, like failing to tell you about a serious credit problem, or falling for a house that there's no way they can afford, or demanding an unreasonable sales price, or insisting on a reduced commission, or worst of all, going out with another agent after you've spent months working with them.

As the old adage goes, s___ happens. And it will happen to you. However, think of your relationship with your seller (or buyer) as being like the relationship with your mother. She's yours, whether right or wrong. Accept it, be as helpful as you possibly can, and move on. Sellers and buyers will often become far more reasonable once they see that you're working with them, not against them. And even loyal clients will sometimes take a dalliance with another agent just to test the waters. Forget, forgive, be helpful, and they'll love you for it.

You Stand Up for What You Believe. There are three no-nos in polite business conversation:

- Politics
- Sex
- Religion

If we're smart, we'll tend to stay away from these three topics, because most people hold strong beliefs on all of them. Start talking about any of these and you can quickly get into a disagreement, which can become a strong argument.

However, if the subject comes up, and you feel a certain way, then you shouldn't first sound out your client's beliefs and then pretend to agree. (This holds true for almost any subject over which you and the client disagree.) Becoming a sycophant is a sure way to lose the trust of others. No one trusts or believes a "yes" man or woman.

Of course, you don't have to insult the other person's views either, and you certainly don't have to try to convert them to yours. When the issue comes up, you can simply and quickly explain your position, not wavering from it, and move on. In most cases, you'll earn the respect of the other person.

You Have a "Shtick." It's an old vaudeville term and is frequently used in show business. Its original meaning was that you had an act that you could fall back upon. If you went on stage, you might be a ventriloquist with a "talking" dog. That was your shtick.

In business a shtick has a different meaning. It's something endearing that you do, besides being just a real estate agent. For example, I know an agent whose shtick is telling only slightly dirty (featuring sex or religion) jokes. I've seen him cull such jokes out of joke books and off the Internet and then use me as a foil when he tried them out. When he was with a seller or buyer, at sometime in the conversation, usually when there was an uncomfortable pause, he would tell a joke. Everyone would laugh, and the tension would be broken. And, because the joke was slightly dirty, everyone felt they had just gotten in on a little secret. And if the joke was particularly clever, the clients (and even other agents) admired him for his wit.

Of course, jokes may not be your cup of tea. One agent I knew read palms and told the future. She was an instant hit, for some reason particularly with women. Bill Clinton, when he was running for office, would often get on stage with a band and play the saxophone. People loved him for it because it revealed a new and charming facet to his personality. If you don't already have a shtick, develop one. If nothing else, it will fill in the uncomfortable pauses in conversation. And if applied judiciously, will make your clients love, or at least like, you.

Reason Number 2 for Selecting You: You Appear to Be Successful to Them

Remember, when people list their house they are entrusting you with what is probably their most valuable asset. They are looking to you to produce satisfying results. They anticipate that you know what you're doing.

And how do you convince clients that you really do know what you're doing?

One way is to wow them with your deep knowledge of real estate practice, although that's just as likely to confuse them. Another is to point to your license and then the additional course work you've taken (from a place such as the Realtor's Institute).

Things such as this help. But what really breaks through is when the client believes you're successful. The reason you can sell their house faster and for money is because you've done it so many times for so many others.

TIP

The only thing that never requires an explanation or an excuse is success.

At some point, if you've convinced a potential seller that you're a success in the field, that you can truly help her, she'll begin thinking that *you're the one.* You're the one person to be "her agent," to take her listing. To find her a home.

But, how do you show your success?

One way is to have a lot of previous listings and sales. You can point to the house down the street that you sold two months ago, the listings on the next block, and another at the other end of the seller's street. You can say that you're the number one listing and sales agent in your office—if it happens to be true. You can tell her (quietly, discreetly) about your success.

TIP

Success is like a closed loop. The more you have it, the more of it you get. It builds and builds on itself.

Give the Appearance of Success

If you can't yet point to your successes, then at the least appear to be successful.

Chances are that if you're just starting out you haven't sold a house on the next street and may not even have any nearby listings. And you might not be number one in your office.

TIP

The next best thing to true success is the appearance of success.

Nevertheless, if you appear to be successful, then clients will begin to believe that you are. There are three rules for appearing to be successful.

1. Always think of yourself as successful. It rubs off

2. Know recent sales like the back of your hand. Memorize all the recent sales prices as well as the special features of those properties. Only someone who's successfully involved in the business could be expected to know so much.

3. Look successful. Chances are you won't be able to drive the finest car when you start, but get a good-looking car that's easy for people to get into and out of. And dress well. Today with stores like Ross, Marshalls, and even Macy's, it doesn't cost a lot to look expensive.

Reason Number 3 for Selecting You: You're Available

Some people think I'm joking when I say this, but it's true. Many a listing and an offer have been lost to someone else because the agent simply wasn't available. When your client wants to make a move, you've got to be there to facilitate it.

Today, there's no reason not to be available. There are cell phones, pagers, faxes, answering machines, e-mail. Anyone on this planet can be reachable, if she or he chooses to be.

TRAP

Loyalty tends to be time-sensitive. When a client who is ready to make a move calls, if you're not available, after a while that client will call someone else.

But, you may argue, what if at that moment you're involved with another client and another deal?

You've got a cell phone, haven't you? (If you don't, get one.) You can call from almost anywhere. Take a momentary time-out from your current business and call the eager client. Explain that you're on another deal and it may take a few hours (or the rest of the day). Assure them that you'll be there ready to service them as soon as humanly possible. Most people will understand and will wait, provided they don't think they're being ignored.

Once you master the three reasons noted above, you should be well on your way to converting leads to listings and buyers to sales.

However, many new agents still feel stymied in getting listings simply because of their inability to say the right thing. Often this happens *after* you've talked to a seller (or for that matter, a buyer). You may think of all sorts of arguments you could have said that would have made a difference. But you just didn't come up with the right words.

When you're just starting out, the hardest thing is to know what to say. What are you going to tell a seller that will result in your getting a listing? What will you say to buyers to get them to make an offer? How are you going to get all the parties to close the deal?

You may know all of the legalities. You may know how to fill out a listing agreement as well as a deposit receipt, but what do you actually *say* to get buyers and sellers to act?

Role-Playing and Scripts

Many trainers advise that you use prewritten *scripts* and *dialogues*. If you haven't heard of these before, you're sure to be quickly introduced to them. In fact, I'm sure they've already been used on you.

For example, someone calls on the phone to sell home insulation. They ask your name and how you're doing. As soon as you respond, any response, they begin talking. They're actually reading from a written script that takes a half minute or so to recite and that ends with them saying something anyone could agree with, such as, "Utility bills are too high, aren't they? Don't you agree with that?"

Since few people disagree, you're expected to say, "Yes." At that point, they continue with the script; they talk about how you can save money on your utilities by insulating your home. And on it goes until you agree to buy.

A great way to sell, right?

Wrong! I don't know about you, but whenever anyone reads from a prepared script, I can tell it. The words sound "canned." My response is to hang up.

In fact, telemarketers who used such scripts over the phone became such a nuisance that the Federal Trade Commission (FTC) created the National Do Not Call Registry, which allows people to opt out of such calls.

Most of the time scripts and dialogues simply don't work. Even if you memorize all the words, every situation is going to be at least somewhat different from every other. And the minute the other party begins to realize you're simply mouthing words designed to manipulate them, you've lost them. If they're polite, they'll excuse themselves and leave. If not, they may tell you to get out in no uncertain terms.

Talking Points: a Better Method

On the other hand, where does that leave you? You still don't know what to say—or do you?

Here's what I suggest. When talking during a listing presentation, instead of memorizing a script word for word, memorize arguments. (In the world of politics and showbiz, these are sometimes called "talking points.") These are arguments that you can use to sway a seller to sign a listing, or to overcome a buyer's objection to a property.

Why use talking points? Think of it this way: Remember that last time you were in a discussion with someone, and only after it was over did you remember your best arguments? Well here, you've memorized your best arguments so that you can more easily access them as the occasion arises.

Typical Arguments (Talking Points).

- It always can be changed to suit your needs. (As in: You can remodel, repaint, recarpet, and so on.)
- Putting off making a decision is still making a decision. (Next week, the house may be gone.)
- The price is only too high if you can't afford it, or don't want it.
- Rate the house in terms of how badly you want it from 1 to 10. If it's 1, then you can easily move on. If it's 10, how can you not buy it?
- You get what you pay for. The reason you should pay a full commission is that I'll provide full service.
- It only seems like the commission is high. Then explain the split.

Know Which Argument to Use, When

Buyers and sellers usually have four different types of reasons for refusing to sign a listing or purchase agreement. They include the following.

An Objection. Here, the client finds something wrong with the property or with the listing agreement. Often you can use arguments to overcome an objection. For example, say that the objection is to the kitchen not being modern enough. You can point out that kitchens can always be modernized. And in doing so, the buyers can get just the appliances, cabinets, countertop, and so on, they want. Besides, an outdated kitchen may warrant a lower offer.

A Demand. Here, the clients are telling you what they want. If they want a three-bedroom home with a swimming pool, and you're showing them four-bedroom homes without a pool, you're wasting your time. Rarely will you be able to overcome a demand. The one time you can is when you convince the clients that they can't get what they want in their price range and, hence, they must eliminate or change their requirement.

A "No." Here, the client is not objecting or demanding, but simply saying, "No." While some sales people never take "no" for an answer, the real solution is to avoid getting into a situation where the client says "No." Often this occurs when the client has decided that he or she simply doesn't want to work with you. See above for clues on avoiding this problem.

A Stall. Here, the client wants to hold off on making a decision. The sellers say that they'll list, but they want to wait a few weeks. They want to see how the market is doing. They want to have time to fix up their existing property. They want to consult with old Aunt Hilda in Colorado. They want to check with another agent. A stall can be overcome if you can convince the client that's it's to his advantage to act immediately. For example, *if it's true,* you can point out that interest rates are rising and that the market's cooling. The longer the seller waits, the less likely she is to get her price.

Watch the Body Language

Look at the other parties' body language to see how your words are going over.

Are their arms crossed in front of their chests in a sign of resistance, or are they sitting relaxed, taking in what you say?

Do they nod in agreement? Or are they silently shaking their heads in opposition?

Watch their hands. Open fists suggest they are going along with what you say. Closed fists suggest resistance. Nervous hands (twitching fingers, opening and closing a fist, tapping fingers on a table) suggest irritation and anxiousness to leave.

Nearly closed, slit eyes suggest a lack of trust in you. Wide open eyes suggest belief.

A relaxed body posture indicates they aren't threatened and may be receptive to what you're saying. A stiff body indicates wariness; they aren't going to want to sign with you.

Don't Jump on the Other Person's Words

Be careful not to speak too quickly. The worst thing you can do is start talking the instant the other person stops. Besides being rude, it conveys the message that you haven't really been listening.

Pause as if you're thinking how to respond, even if you already know how you'll respond. It lets the other party sense that you're seriously considering what they said and are working on coming up with a suitable reply.

Use a Mirror

A long time ago I was a teaching assistant in a college. (I was working my way through school.) I was asked to read business students' papers and make suggestions that would help students write more effectively.

I worked hard at it for several weeks, to no end. I could help them improve spelling, but not their reasoning or their context … until I hit upon an idea that worked very well. I wrote on each of their papers that for their next assignment, they had to read their paper aloud in front of a mirror, then rewrite it.

A simple task, eh? Yet, the papers improved dramatically almost overnight.

Try it. Take a script that you get from a trainer, a book, your broker, or that you write yourself. Now, go into a room by yourself and read it to a mirror.

Suddenly, you'll see exactly what other people see. For perhaps the first time, you'll begin to see how you come across. You'll see how "canned" the script is. You'll see why others haven't been responding to you the way you want.

You should also begin to see points about your presentation that you like. Perhaps you've got a winning smile. You'll want to smile more.

Perhaps you've got a soft way of speaking that causes people to stop and listen. You'll want to stop shouting.

Most of all, when you're looking into the mirror, you can't be reading the script, so you have to come up with your own words of the moment. Oh, yes, you'll still be able to remember the general arguments (talking points) that you had (see above). But, the words will be your own.

As soon as you do this, you've made the first steps from being a tongue-tied beginner to becoming a producing agent.

Closing

Knowledge isn't really one of the big items that's going to convince others to list, or make an offer, with you. Rather, what convinces them are the far more subtle things we've talked about above, particularly their liking and trusting you. But, you won't get that listing or that offer without some knowledge.

You must know what you're doing. Even if you've never taken a listing before or never written up an offer, you must look as though you've done it a thousand times.

TRAP

If your client begins to suspect that you're not quite sure what you're doing, or even worse, that they know more than you, the listing or the deal is lost.

Some newcomers will go out with a more experienced agent (or a mentor) who can sometimes slip in here and handle the paperwork. But it's far better if you do it yourself.

This means that you need to be knowledgeable from the get-go in at least the following areas:

- Pricing
- Financing
- Forms (filling out listing and deposit receipt forms)
- Giving the seller advice on preparing the property for sale

Pricing

On every listing presentation, be prepared to offer a comparative market analysis, or CMA. This is a list of all the recent sales of comparable properties along with their descriptions (square footage, rooms, lot size, features, and so on). This is what helps the seller determine the price. You can readily get all this information from the MLS.

TIP

Be sure you do get your CMA ready beforehand so you can look professional at the listing presentation.

When the seller asks how much the house should sell for (often after already tentatively deciding to list with you), you whip out your CMA sheet. If you're fortunate, it's a good-looking presentation sheet, although many older brokers will simply print out a worksheet from their Excel or other program (which does *not* look that professional).

There should be a place for you to write in the seller's name and phone number as well as the property address. Do *not* preprint this. It looks more immediate if you write it in.

Explain how the CMA works, and why it's useful in determining the price of property. (The seller's home should be worth roughly what similar neighboring houses have sold for.)

Allow time for the information to sink in. At cocktail parties, the seller may have heard fantastic tales of high prices in the neighborhood. Now, you're presenting the real facts. That house up the street the seller thought sold for $550,000 actually sold for only $500,000. The seller now needs to adjust his or her thinking about price.

When the seller asks, "How much should my house sell for?" don't simply pop out with a number, even if you know it. Instead, point to the CMA and go through the numbers. Conclude with, "Based on the comparables, your house should bring $xxx." This way you're not asking the seller to simply take the number on faith. You're showing exactly how you arrived at it. This information is far more difficult to argue with.

Don't Forget About "Future Pricing"

To look really professional (and to get it right), next explain to the seller about trends. If the market has been trending upward at 10 percent a year (a figure you should be able to back up with news reports or information from a statistical service such as www.dataquick.com), and it's been six months since the comps sold, explain that the seller's house may actually be worth about 5 percent more than the CMA suggests (half a year's worth of price appreciation).

The seller will be delighted to hear this news, and think of you as all the more professional. On the other hand, if prices have been trending downward and the seller's home is now 5 percent less than the comps, the seller's reception may be less enthusiastic. Nevertheless, you need to point this trend out in order to get a realistically priced listing (meaning one that will sell and bring you a commission).

Financing

You'll need to know about financing primarily with buyers, unless the seller is carrying paper (usually in the form of a second mortgage). However, today you don't need to be an expert. Just be sure your buyer sees a good mortgage broker and gets pre-approved. A good pre-approval letter should tell you exactly the mortgage size and monthly payment the buyer can afford, at a given interest rate. That way you can show the buyer appropriate properties

TIP

Not all pre-approval letters are alike. Try to get one that's issued by an actual lender and that gives a commitment based on not only a credit report but also on an underwriting analysis. You want this assurance to avoid unpleasant surprises later on, as when, say, it turns out that a pre-approval letter isn't really all it's cracked up to be and the buyer really can't qualify. In such a situation, you would have wasted a lot of your valuable time.

If your seller is carrying back paper (a first or second mortgage), then explain how this is handled in escrow, the interest rate to be expected, what qualifications to request from potential buyers, and how much down to insist upon to protect the seller. If you're a newcomer and don't yet know about secondary paper, get a more experienced agent or your mentor or the client's lawyer to explain it. Or, if he or she isn't available (or doesn't know), be sure that you mention that an expert from your office will explain it. Don't try explaining something that you yourself don't understand. You'll get caught at it most times, and you will look foolish.

TRAP

The trouble with not knowing about seller financing is that the seller may not want to sign the listing agreement until everything is spelled out and explained (a reasonable request). Any delays in signing, however, could ultimately result in a lost listing. Thus, it's worth your while to become an expert on secondary financing. (Check into my book, *How to Get Started in Real Estate Investing*, published by McGraw-Hill.)

Forms

You know all about the deposit receipt, right? So when the seller asks if he should agree to a liquidated damages clause with regard to the deposit (now included in most deposit receipts), you know exactly how to advise him, right? (I find the best way to handle it is to explain what it is and advise the seller that he should contact his attorney for advice. Most sellers, however, will go ahead and make a decision on their own.) Or if the seller wants to add a "subject to" clause (contingency) regarding limits to her payment for termite damage (sellers normally pay for correcting existing termite damage) to $1,000, you know how to handle it, right?

Or when the seller balks at your office's "administrative fee" of $500, you can explain why it's necessary. Or when the seller wants to exclude that exceptionally ugly chandelier from the listing, you know how to write it up, right? (I find the best way is to have the seller remove the chandelier and hang a cheap replacement so you don't need to mention it at all in the listing or sales agreement.)

I'm sure you get the idea. Correctly filling out the forms is a very important part of what you do as an agent. It can mean the difference between a clean deal and a lawsuit, between getting your commission … and not getting it.

It takes years and more than a few bad experiences to learn how to properly fill out the deposit receipt and listing agreement. But even if you're new, you should be able to handle at least the basics.

TIP

Try this exercise. Get a stack of unused listing agreements and deposit receipts. (Your broker should have these readily available.) Then call up some old MLS listings and, based on what the listing says, fill out the forms. Actually write them out, including the names, property address, dates, and so on. Then have a more experienced agent or a mentor or an attorney check them out for correctness. It won't take but a few hours over a couple of days, and it will give you the experience you need to get started.

General Knowledge

Sellers usually will also want to know your take on the current real estate market. Are prices getting higher or lower? How long will current trends continue? How long will it take to sell their house? Having the answers at hand will impress them and go a long way toward cementing the listing or the offer. Here's where to get the information you need.

Getting Current Information

Trend Reports. Real estate Web sites such as www.inman.com, www.realtor.org, and www.robertirwin.com offer opinions on the market. Opinions and insights are also available from local newspapers (search back issues at the newspapers' Internet sites). The government also offers much information on this subject (www.hud.com, www.treasury.com, www.fanniemae.com).

TRAP

Do not make predictions! You could be wrong, yet held to them later in a court of law. Instead, only give opinions and those based only on solid research; for example: "According to the Treasury Department Bulletin, #xxxx, interest rates may be expected to climb in the near future." Many agents always preface opinions with a statement to the effect that, "No one knows the future …" Or, "It's impossible to say with any certainty …"

Timing Report. "How long will it take to sell my house?" If you say, "I'll guarantee it will be sold within a month," what if it doesn't sell? Now not only will the lister be angry, but he or she may also want to take legal action against you, claiming they listed with you only because of what you guaranteed with regard to timing.

Instead, the MLS in your area should provide inventory reports. These include how many are houses on the market at any given time and how long it takes the average house to sell. You can quote these reports. Of course, it's a good idea to begin by saying that buyers are fickle and no one can know with certainty how long it will take to sell any house.

But, you may ask yourself, won't this make the seller think I really don't want to commit to anything? That I'm wishy-washy? That I don't know?

Not usually. Most sellers are realistic. They would rather have the agent truthfully tell them the facts about how long it will take to sell than make unrealistic sounding promises. Promise a quick sale and you chance losing your credibility.

Getting the Signature on the Dotted Line

As you get more experienced, you'll instinctively know when a seller is ready to sign a listing and a buyer to sign an offer. However, until you feel confident, my suggestion is that you ask. After you've made your presentation, at some point simply ask, "Shall we go ahead and list your property?" Or, "Shall we make the offer?"

While it's true that if you ask too often or too early you could scare away a seller or buyer, a newcomer is much more likely to miss the listing or the offer by failing to ask at all. I've seen agents talk a seller into listing and then continue on until they've talked him out of it.

If you're unsure when they're ready to sign, ask. You might have to ask two or three times during the presentation before you get the nod. Then, it's on to filling out the form and getting the signatures.

8

Everything You Need to Know About Buyers

"Buyers are not liars."

Probably the most frequently heard maxim regarding home purchasers is that they don't tell the truth. "Buyers are liars," in fact, has become part of the vernacular of many real estate agents, at least when they speak among themselves. When asked, many can tell you striking examples of lost deals to prove their case.

The trouble is that not only is this statement false, it also covers up a bigger problem, namely that many real estate agents simply don't understand buyers. It's sort of like saying that children are liars. While it's true that many children do tell an occasional fib, they usually do so because in certain circumstances they are afraid of telling the truth. Something similar holds with buyers.

Once you understand what motivates buyers and where they are really coming from, you'll understand why they may tell the occasional fib, or more commonly, may simply leave out vital bits of information. Understand buyers and respond to their true needs, and almost all will shine with veracity.

From the Buyer's Perspective

Today's real estate market deals with big numbers. A modest house in Los Angeles or Boston, for example, can cost at least half a million dollars. Nationwide as of this writing the median price for a home is nearly a quarter million dollars. Thus, when you're talking to a buyer about making a purchase, the sums involved are huge, at least the way most people look at money. Thus, there's bound to be some resistance on the part of most buyers to talk with you about the figures.

TRAP

Before making a home purchase, most buyers have only talked about sums over $100,000 in confidence with their most trusted banker or financial advisor. Is it any wonder they are reluctant to discuss the matter with a real estate agent they met 30 minutes ago?

Add to this the stereotypical conception of real estate agents that most buyers have, and you have a mix that makes for suspicion.

What's the Stereotype of the Typical Real Estate Agent?

Who are the most trusted people in America? Studies have shown that right up there at the top are doctors, ministers, and airline pilots. But, turn the list around and look at the bottom and what do you find? Rightly or wrongly—it's often used-car salespeople, lawyers, and real estate agents.

This may come as a shock to many who an entering the profession. Many of those who become agents don't have a feel for how the general public regards them. But, take a tip from me, in general you are not going to be highly regarded.

Why is that? Why the low esteem for agents who, in truth, are regulated in every state, who in the vast majority of cases are honest and ethical, and who perform a valuable service for their clients? Why the disconnect?

How Buyers See You

I've found that a large part of the problem comes from the anticipation that buyers have that their agent is going to try and pressure them to buy something they don't want and may not be able to afford. This is the mindset that many, perhaps most, buyers bring to the table when they first meet you.

It comes in part from the fact that today almost all buyers know that you aren't going to get paid unless and until they make a purchase. Therefore, right from the get-go, you and everything you say is under suspicion. Are you telling them this is the perfect house for them because it is? Or are you just saying it because you want them to buy quickly so you can collect a commission? While you have a clear fiduciary responsibility to act for their benefit (certainly you do if you're their agent), your own pocketbook may be telling a different story.

Used-car salespeople have a similar image problem. At one time, horror stories of high-pressure salespeople were rampant. I personally was once victimized by a salesman borrowing my old car keys, ostensibly to move the car out of an active driveway, and then throwing the keys on the roof of the building so I couldn't leave until I bought. Others commonly speak of being traded off from one used-car salesperson to another until the buyers couldn't remember what deal they had been offered or what they wanted. Many finally bought just out of frustration and exhaustion.

I'm sure that doesn't happen anymore, except in rare cases. Car dealerships have been working hard to upgrade their image, particularly in the case of high-end automobiles, where there is virtually no pressure to buy at all.

Nevertheless, old stories are told, and old perceptions are hard to change. The same applies to real estate.

Years ago I actually knew an agent who would take clients out in his car and keep showing them houses even after they asked to be taken back to the office. He would insist they buy something, and he always refused to take them back. Exhausted, many clients would finally sign a purchase agreement.

Such a scenario is unheard of today. Such an agent would lose his or her license in a heartbeat. Nevertheless, old stories die hard, as do old biases.

Thus, when you're out with buyers, chances are you're under suspicion. The buyers are watching you carefully: how you act, what you say. They are looking for certain tip-offs that will alert them to your good—or bad—intentions.

What Buyers Are Suspicious of When First Meeting an Agent

- Any sort of high-pressure tactic that insists they choose a house or make an offer, *now*.

- Any line of questioning that asks buyers how much money they have, what they want to spend, and what payments they can afford. (Buyers feel this way even though this is basic information you must have to properly qualify them.)

- Any sort of demand for commitment on the buyers' part regarding loyalty to you.

- Any questioning regarding how committed the buyers are to another agent.

- Any questions asking how soon the buyers are ready to act, whether they've sold their current home, whether it's already listed, and so on.

In other words, because of preconceptions, many buyers are going to be suspicious of you, even though you ask good questions so you can try to do your job in the best way possible. Let's consider an example.

Meeting a Buyer at an Open House

You're working an open house for another agent and hope to get prospects out of it. Would-be buyers come by, and you welcome them. They smile, but they are hesitant to give you even their names. But you shake their hands, give them your full name, and hand them a business card. So, what can they do? They tell you they are Pat and Jerry Smith.

TIP

Until they know you better, buyers are going to be resistant to give you any information at all, even their names. However, once you have their names, you've made the first step toward establishing rapport. *Never* speak at length to anyone until you've introduced yourself and they've reciprocated.

Now you ask them how soon they're interested in buying, right?

Wrong! They know you 30 seconds, and already you want to know about their buying goals. So, they tell you a little fib. They say they are only looking and have no intentions of buying soon. (These often are the buyers who make an offer on another house that same day.) Or, they say they are red hot to buy. (These frequently are the buyers who are just passing time before showing up at a party an hour later in the same neighborhood, who love to tour open houses and watch agents react when they push the right buttons.)

When you learn the truth, as eventually you very well may, you begin to think, "Buyers are liars!"

Yes, they've told fibs. But only because you pushed them into it. You weren't close enough, didn't have enough rapport with them, before you asked them a personal question. It was *you* who set yourself up to be lied to.

Instead of asking a question, perhaps you welcome them to the open house. Maybe you offer them some cookies. You hand them a sheet that describes the house. You give them its square footage. You tell them its price. You outline its special features. You tell them to look around.

Then, you talk about housing prices in the neighborhood, you explain your own interests in real estate (and point out you live nearby, if you do). You begin talking about how easy it is to finance a house today, how this house's seller is willing to carry back paper (if the seller is). And so on.

Along the way, chances are the buyers will *volunteer* how close they are to buying a property, what price range they are looking at, what they find wrong with the current home, what they are looking for, and so on.

By the end of the conversation, if handled properly, you and they are, if not close friends, at least real estate collaborators. They are looking for a specific house at a specific price point—and you just happen to know of such a house only half a mile away. Would they like to see it?

Before you get to your first question, if handled well, the buyers have volunteered virtually everything you need to know to qualify them.

Does It Really Work That Way?

Ideally, it does work this way. However, many experienced agents will tell you that since most of those coming to an open house are just lookers, you'll spend a lot of wasted time devoting so much energy to every person walking through the door. My response is, what are you there to do, if not engage people in conversation, establish rapport, and *make contact?* You've got an afternoon to spend. Why not spend it talking to people the whole time? If you talk to 15 people and only one pans out as a real buyer, to whom you eventually sell a property, you've won! On the other hand, if you simply drive away prospects with your eagerness (which they interpret as pressure tactics) or what's worse, remain mute and come away with no solid lead, you've lost.

TRAP

Don't be afraid to chat with everyone. You never really know which person is the solid lead and which is the "looker." Just because people, at first, say they really aren't interested in buying any time soon, doesn't mean that they won't buy tomorrow. And don't ever show that you are upset with people who don't immediately pan out. To do so only means that you'll never develop them into solid prospects later on. Remember, people with whom you talk are not there to help you make a commission. You're there to help them find the right house. Your job is to provide service, not make demands.

Other Reasons Buyers Will Fib to You

People will fib for many other reasons as well.

High-Pressure Tactics

One reason that people will lie is high-pressure tactics. I once knew an agent who would "qualify" buyers before ever taking them out to see a house. He would say something like, "I'm the top agent in this office. I got to this position by not wasting my time or my clients' time. Houses in my area sell for between $500,000 and $600,000. If you can't afford that, then there's no point looking.

"If we go looking, I'll show you the best five houses on the market. One of them will be just right for you. I'll help you buy it. But, if you decide not to buy one of those five, I won't take you again, because you'd be wasting my time and yours. You decide right now whether or not you're really a buyer. If you are, let's tour some houses. If not, I have real clients waiting."

Quite a speech, isn't it? I almost choked when I first heard him present it. About three-fourths of those prospects he told too, simply left, most feeling insulted. The remaining fourth went out with him and, in truth, he sold a fair amount of houses. However, others in the office also sold many houses, often to those who had walked out on the high-pressure agent.

In other words, many buyers simply left, not because they weren't buyers, but because they recognized a high-pressure tactic and responded to it negatively.

Commitment to Other Agents

Sometimes a prospect will come in over the transom or at an open house or from a phone call asking about a particular listing your office has. You strike up a conversation, seeking to establish rapport.

TIP

The key to converting prospects to buyers is to get close to them, to establish rapport so they confide and trust in you.

The trouble is that if these are real buyers, chances are they are already working with another agent. Indeed, they may have gone out to see homes with the other agent a half dozen times and are committed to working with him or her.

Somewhere during the conversation, usually when you offer to take them to see the property (or sometimes later on), they may admit they are working with another agent. If this happens, you now are presented with an ethical dilemma. Do you say something like, "Oh, it's okay, we work with other agents all the time." Which probably means that if they buy through you, chances are that ultimately the other agent will get nothing.

Or, do you bite the bullet and say, "Then perhaps you should have your agent show you the house."

If you choose the first road, you are basically "stealing" a prospect. If you choose the second, you are acting in a highly ethical manner, which could cost you a commission— or make you one (see below).

The real problem, for you, occurs when these would-be buyers don't tell you of a commitment they have to another agent. Rather, they let you show them the property, then later on they make an offer through another agent. And you end up convinced that "buyers are liars."

Can you claim a portion of the commission for showing the property to them first? Maybe, but it can get ugly, particularly if the buyers won't vouch for you.

A better approach is to explain up-front to buyers how the relationship between them and an agent works. Explain that whoever first shows them the property may be entitled to a commission. Then you can politely ask reticent buyers if they are working with another agent. Presented with this question, most will respond honestly and you'll know up-front what the situation is.

They may admit they are working with another agent through whom they will make any offers, and go their way. Or, as frequently happens, they will say something like, "Oh, but we'd much rather work with you. We don't want to work with that other agent anymore. He simply hasn't shown us anything we like!"

If this happens and they are sincere, then you're probably clear to work with these prospects, although you should advise them to contact the other agent and let him know what's happened. You may want to be sure by calling the other agent yourself as well, although the outcome certainly will be better if they call first.

Dealing with prospects who are committed to another agent is simply spinning your wheels. You'll spend time, gas, and energy with them, all to no avail when another agent comes in with the deal. Be up-front with the prospect about how showing property works, and chances are they'll be up-front with you.

Uncommitment to Themselves

There is yet another problem that leads to agent's frustration, the fact that buyers may not even know what they want. A buyer may tell you she wants a five-bedroom house, only to later buy a three-bedroom home. A buyer may demand a view lot, only to settle for an interior unit in a condo.

Are these and buyers in similar situations all lying to you? Or is it the case that they simply don't know their own minds?

An experienced agent will recognize early on that buyers need to be educated. They need to know what's on the market, what it costs, and how much they can afford and truly need. Many prospects who come to you lack any of this information. So, much of your work will be to inform them. You're part agent—and part teacher. Overlook the teacher part, and suddenly it might appear that your prospects are lying. Teach them, and they'll become truthful.

Cementing the Relationship

If you haven't been in the following situation, you probably soon will be. You meet some prospects who indicate they are anxious to buy a home. You spend a while talking to them, qualifying them. You set up an appointment for a few days later, and they promise to meet you, ready to buy. So, you go out scouting, looking for properties that they might like.

A few days later you show them five homes. Unfortunately, none is quite right. So you arrange to meet with them the following weekend to go looking again. You scout out another bunch of houses and prepare a list of six more to show them. On Friday you call to confirm the meeting on Saturday, and they inform you that they bought a house you didn't show them from another agent last Wednesday.

What happened to buyer loyalty? What happened to truthfulness? What about all that work you did running around looking for houses for them? Why are buyers so unfaithful and treacherous?

TRAP

Many agents consider the term "buyer's loyalty" an oxymoron. It simply doesn't exist. That's an unfortunate misreading of buyer's intent.

The Game of Buyers

Perhaps the best way of understanding why buyers appear to be disloyal is to think of it as a kind of game, a game in which *you* start out with 100 points. In this game, however, you can't ever get any more points. And the minute you start playing you lose points ... until you lose the game. Let's analyze the previous example in terms of this game:

You make contact with prospects and impress them with your knowledge of the field and your dedication to helping them. After a while they like you (even if they don't yet love you—see previous chapter).

So you spend a few days scouring the MLS for possible homes that might suit them. Then, you spend an entire weekend days taking them out in your car, spending your gas money, maybe even paying for their lunch. (This is a "no-no" for most agents, although it can be worthwhile with good clients.)

Now, they should be in your debt, right? They should be loyal to you for all that time, effort, and even money you spent on them, right?

Wrong! From the buyers' perspective, you've turned out to be a loser! You first impressed them with how much you'd be able to help them find a house. Then you showed them five or six houses that weren't right for them.

From their perspective, you have done the following:

- Wasted their time
- Weren't able to show them the right house
- Demonstrated that you really don't know as much about real estate as you said you did.

Take 25 points away from the 100 you started with. Now, in the buyers' minds you're down to 75 points.

Yes, perhaps they'll forgive you for your failures and go out with you the next weekend. But, if you show them half a dozen more houses and still none of them are right, you're down to 50 points. A third weekend and you're down to 25 points. How long do you think buyers are going to hang around you the way you're losing points? Is it any wonder that they call other agents, that they go out with other agents?

In the Game of Buyers, the more work and time you, the agent, put into the prospects, the more your credibility suffers and the less loyal buyers are likely to be to you.

So, what do you do about this?

Rebuilding Your Credibility

In a courtroom, after the other attorney has cross-examined an attorney's witness, he or she has an opportunity to go back and attempt to rebuild that witness, to gain back the original credibility he or she had with the jury. The same thing must be done after every *unsuccessful* showing.

You must now go over all of the same things you originally did to win the prospects' confidence. You must give reasons why you were unable to show them the right house; you must reemphasize your knowledge of the market; you must point out any special needs they have that make finding the right house more difficult.

Most important, you must be like a good mother and lay a guilt trip on them. You may point out all the work you did, without making it seem like their fault—it was your job to do it. You may point out all the work you're going to do before you next show them houses— again, emphasizing that it's just your job. It sometimes helps to subtly point out that you're *gladly* doing all this because you know they'll eventually buy through you and you'll get a commission.

It also helps to tell them that if they drive by a home they like, or read about one in the paper, or on the Internet, to immediately call you *anytime* day or night. You'll instantly get them all the inside information on it and show it to them. This will save them the trouble of starting all over again with a new agent.

TRAP

Many otherwise good agents fail to remind their prospects to call them whenever they want to get information on a house. Yes, this is inconvenient for the agent, but buyers who don't get information right when they want it from you will get it from someone else: your competitor. Be sure you have a cell phone, always carry it with you and have it charged, and give its number to your prospects.

After a *failed* showing, you may be able to rebuild your image. But remember that in the Game of Buyers you can never get back to 100 points. Work on your image, and you may get back to 90 points, or if you're lucky, back to 95, but never to 100. However, that's a whole lot better than falling to 75 points. It means you can keep working with these prospects for a while longer.

How to Keep Buyers Loyal

What should be obvious is in the Game of Buyers, loyalty is not earned in the usual way. Work hard, spend days searching for the right houses to show, take buyers on a tour of homes that you hope will fit their needs—but don't, and they'll look at you as a failure. On the other hand, find them the house that they want and they'll call you a genius, tout your talents to others (giving you solid leads), and call you up again when it's time for them to sell.

TIP

The one thing that never needs an excuse is success. Find buyers a home they can live with and they'll reward you with a purchase ... and a commission.

When dealing with buyers, the following are five secrets I've found that will help you keep them loyal to you.

Secrets of Keeping Buyers Loyal

- *Never complain about all the behind-the-scenes work you do.* You can mention it and point out that you're happy to do it, but don't try to make them feel obligated because of it. Doing that will only backfire.

- *Always remind buyers of your expertise in real estate.* Convince them that you're the best agent for them. Make them love or at least like you (see previous Chapter).

- *Outperform your competitors.* Buyers are quick to see who really works for them and who doesn't. Do the work, take credit for it, but make it seem easy. If buyers see you as the best agent around, why would they want to go to another?

- *Never get mad at buyers.* When they seem disloyal, remember, that is only happening because of something you did, or failed to do. Getting mad at buyers will drive them away. Getting mad at yourself should help you to do better next time. (Be realistic. Don't tell buyers you know just the right house for them. You can't know that. Tell them you can show them houses that will fit their needs and their wants. Then, if they don't like the place, it's their fault, not yours.)

TIP

Never promise what you can't deliver, but always deliver more than you promise.

9

Tools of the Trade

The squeamish need not apply—becoming a successful real estate agent is a full-contact sport. Unlike other professionals who may pass the hours behind a desk, real estate agents are up, out, and running across town. Some days agents may be required to zip around the neighborhood showing different houses while others may require that they solicit leads door to door. There are a million and one different activities that a top agent will engage in, and constant movement is a near necessity. But do not fear, there are tools of the trade that can drastically improve your efficiency and help reduce the intensity of agent life.

Unlike handymen and their tool belts or architects and their rulers, agents vary in the type and quantity of tools they use on the job. There is no toolbox handed out on the first day, and yet there is no way to be successful without relying on a few devices throughout your career.

TIP

Your success as a real estate agent will be less influenced by the types of tools you decide to use than by the way in which you use them. As is true elsewhere in life, playing smartly trumps playing loudly.

Your Chariot

The first and foremost tool that any real estate agent must have is a reliable car. (Note, the word *reliable* is not a superfluous adjective!) You will likely log more hours in your car after the first three months on the job than you did the previous year. Some of this time will be spent driving solo through your farm or on caravan (when agents tour new listings), but much of the time will be driving clients from house to house. While you may have never spent much time worrying about the condition of your vehicle in the past, you can be certain it will make an impression on your clients. To ensure that this impression is a positive one, remember the following tips.

Four Is Better Than Two

If debating what kind of car to buy, remember that, for the real estate agent, four doors are better than two. The logic is simple. For example, suppose you are going to be showing a couple around; you will want to make it easy for the person sitting in back to get in and out of the car.

The point is even more obvious when you consider the likelihood of showing a family of three, four, or even five around for a day. You may also find yourself showing homes to individuals who may find it physically challenging to get into and out of a two-door vehicle. In almost no circumstances will you be worse off with a four-door car.

Keep It Clean

No one wants to deal with someone else's mess. As obvious as this statement may sound, too often this rule is ignored. But beware! Even beyond the grossness, having an unkempt car suggests that you are sloppy in all things you do. I once knew an agent whose car had a miserable smell. Is this the type of person with whom a homebuyer would feel comfortable managing a transaction involving hundreds of thousands of dollars?

Gas It Up

While you are not a taxi, you also aren't leisurely driving friends around town. Respect your clients' time, and avoid unnecessary stops like getting gas while showing homes.

Log Your Miles

Each mile driven as part of the job is likely to be a deductible item on your taxes. Definitely log your miles and keep track of gas spent. When it comes time to file, check with your accountant to see if you are eligible to deduct miles, gas, or both.

Map It

Don't get lost! This used to be an inevitable part of the job, but it no longer is. Today it is quite easy to install a global positioning system (GPS) in your car. Using the live directions, you can be sure to never (or almost never) get lost.

You don't have to buy a GPS if you don't want it. However, not having one is no excuse to get lost with a client in the car. Check and recheck the map and address to ensure that you know how to get where you're going.

Get the Best Car You Can

Yes, cars are expensive. But, the tools you use will determine the work you turn out. And your car can be your number-one tool. Besides, agents typically get significant tax breaks when buying or leasing a car; check with your accountant to see whether you're eligible.

TIP

Even if your car did not originally come with a GPS built in, you can add one for a few hundred dollars. Depending on your needs and familiarity with the local streets, this purchase can be an excellent one.

Marketing

As any one who has sat through a commercial break during prime-time television knows, marketing is paramount to selling. While you may not be peddling something as tangible as in the commercials, you are nonetheless selling.

A successful marketing strategy will tap into several different channels. (A channel simply refers to a way in which you transmit information.) Following are a few different channels and a couple of tips for how to best integrate them in your arsenal of tools.

Yard Signs

The most uniformly accepted channel for advertising a house for sale is a yard sign. The sign, often provided or specified by your office, will send a signal to anyone driving or walking by that the house is for sale. In addition, the sign will often include personal information about you or your office so that someone not interested in that particular home can still contact you for more information.

Business Cards

Business cards are great for many reasons. First, they are small and versatile, and they will save you from searching for a pen in order to give someone your contact information. Second, they enable you to provide several different ways for someone to reach out to you (for example, phone number, e-mail address, and street address). Finally, they are great keepsakes for someone who may not immediately need information but who may want to refer to you later.

For all of the above reasons, it is very wise to invest in a set of business cards. Your office may provide you with their standard business card, but you can usually do better on your own. The cards do not need to be especially expensive (although, as a rule, avoid anything that is particularly flimsy or too flashy). A good business card will provide all of the necessary information about you and your office and be easy to read.

Many real estate agents also prefer to put their picture on a business card. This, in my opinion, is a personal decision, but it can be an excellent way of having a client remember you. Often people may forget a name before they'll forget a face.

Finally, remember that a business card doesn't do you any good if it's sitting in your desk drawer. Always remember to carry a set of business cards and hand them out whenever you see the opportunity.

Flyers

There are many kinds of flyers. One type gives vital information about a listing as well as a picture of the house for sale; you'll want to have such flyers in a little box on your sign for customers to pick up at any time.

Another type of flyer is the kind you hand out or mail out that gives information on you, the market, homes recently sold, and so on. These are typically sent to an area that you are farming.

Keep in mind that flyers need not be expensive or difficult to create. They can be put together easily with a word processing program on your own computer. You can even print them out on your printer, although making copies at a copy store is usually the faster, cheaper, and easier way to go. A one-page flyer that uses both front and back sides is usually sufficient, particularly if it includes one or more pictures in color.

Remember that people are used to getting junk mail, and you are therefore starting at a disadvantage. Here are a couple of tips to make your flyer "sexier" to the prospective client.

- *Add a picture.* Put your picture on the front. It will help to personalize the statement you are making, and it will provide the reader with an insight into the person who wrote the flyer.

- *Use color.* Simply printing on color paper is a low-cost way to make your flyer more attractive. (But keep in mind that using color text or pictures can quickly become expensive. You may want to reserve this option unless you have the budget.)

- *Use catchy headlines.* People immediately jump to the bold print on the page, so make sure you use headlines that grab attention.

- *Provide local information.* People will most be interested in reading the flyer if it tells them something new and relevant. The most common item is to list recent home sales and prices, which usually become public information after the sale is concluded. People love to see what other homes in their area have sold for. Also, consider adding things like information about the local market, interesting neighborhood facts, local restaurants, even a favorite recipe. The goal is to provide something provocative enough to merit the reader putting your flyer on the refrigerator door.

Web Site

It is becoming increasingly hard to avoid the Internet and, these days, it is almost a requirement for a real estate agent to have a Web site. Make sure your site is consistent with the image you are trying to make for yourself through all the other channels. Also, make sure you keep your Web site current. (See more about Web sites in Chapter 10.)

Working Open Houses

The open house is at the heart of an agent's toolbox, as described in Chapter 5. Remember that beyond the goal of selling the subject's house, your own goal is to get new clients, buyers, and sellers. To that end, try using the following methods.

Keep a visitors list. Be sure to capture contact information, if possible, for everyone who attends the open house. Remember, potential clients may be more willing to give out an e-mail address than a phone number. As described in Chapter 5, these may be some of your best leads. It's also for general security for any property that may be jeopardized during the showing. Further, the person who signs the roll, in some cases, may be considered your client if she or he later buys through another agent. Get a special book, readily available at stationery stores, that has columns for name, address, phone, e-mail, and so on.

Hand out business cards and flyers. An open house is a perfect time to hand out the business cards and flyers that you've prepared. This is where having your picture on the flyer and the card can help the client remember to whom he or she has talked.

Offer to send more information. People who attend an open house will almost never refuse your offer to send more information to them. Now you've got their permission to make further contact. And, if you're using a good roll book, you'll be able to mail or e-mail to them more information on homes in the area. At this point, taking notes on what they are looking for is most important. In addition to the roll book, keep your own PDA or notes on each person who comes through.

Cell Phones, Digital Cameras, Computers, PDAs, Oh My!

It seems there is virtually no end to the variety of technology devices today. If you wanted, you could easily fill every one of your pockets with a phone, PDA, satellite radio, digital camera, computer, and so on. And while most of these devices are fun toys, they come with a cost. It is important to determine which devices will make you more efficient as a top real estate agent and which ones are best left on the shelf.

Cell Phones

These are indispensable. Long ago are the days of land lines and occasional cell phones. In fact, things have evolved so much that we often see the opposite: people forgo land lines and depend solely on their portable phones. The convenience and falling prices of cell phones have won the hearts of most people. Perhaps more than for most professionals, real estate agents almost certainly need a cell phone.

No doubt being an agent is a technical job requiring area expertise, but at the root of the real estate agent's value added is service. The real estate agent can provide the most expertise as an advisor and specialist. Of course, this is assuming he or she can be reached. The cell phone enables clients to reach you no matter where you are or what you are doing.

Take your cell phone with you at all times, but be conscious of your surroundings. If you enter a delicate meeting with a client who is considering several serious offers, consider putting your phone on silence or shutting it off entirely. Also you may want to pick a subtle ringer that is not too loud or annoying.

If your business cell phone number is the same as your personal cell phone number, be sure to create a professional voicemail and one that you wouldn't mind clients hearing.

Digital Cameras

Another useful device is the digital camera. While not as mandatory as a cell phone, the digital camera can be quite useful. Obviously you can use the camera to take snapshots of a home to create a for-sale flyer as well as to put up on your Web site. However, there are a few other ways in which the device will come in handy.

Video notebook. When showing clients several properties in a given day, you can easily use your digital camera to snap the front of each house (or another unique feature) to help keep them all fresh in the potential buyers' minds. You can even print a photo keepsake when you get back to the office for your clients to take with them.

E-mail/Web Site updates. Another use for the digital camera is sending digital pictures over the Internet to clients and other agents. And as noted, it can be quite easy to post pictures to your Web site as well.

Again, the digital camera is probably not an absolute necessity, although it is very useful. They have become quite inexpensive, costing around one or two hundred dollars. It is quite likely that someone else in your office can loan you a camera in a worst-case scenario.

Personal Computer

For the purposes of this section we will assume that your office will have a computer available for your use. If the answer is no or you are not affiliated with an office, you should definitely consider purchasing a computer in the very near future.

Although newcomers to the industry may find it hard to imagine, at one time the norm used to be that real estate agents worked without a computer and used exclusively an MLS listing book that was published weekly. Times have certainly changed, and the computer is as pervasive as a number-two pencil. The question is not whether you need a computer or not. (The answer is most definitely "yes"!) The real question is, do you need your own personal machine?

The answer will depend on a number of things. One to consider is how comfortable are you with using various applications. For some, the thought of using a word processing program is more painful than a pen and pad of paper. If you are one of these people, then the office desktop will likely suffice.

Another thing to consider is the many software tools that are available for download or over the Web which make the real estate agent's life a little easier. For example, there are great programs for calculating monthly mortgage payments based on the mortgage type and down payment information. You can also generate paperwork quite easily from templates available online. But perhaps the most useful is using the Web to search listings. With just a few clicks you can get a ton of information about a particular house, neighborhood, or city. All this is to say that there are excellent computer resources available to the technically adroit agent.

TIP

Computers can vary dramatically in cost and functionality. You can probably find a computer that suits your needs without buying the latest and greatest model. Be considerate of your financial constraints before you commit to an expensive machine.

PDAs

PDA stands for personal digital assistant which, more often than not, is nothing more than a fancy term for an organizer. Two common PDAs are the Palm Pilot and Blackberry. Each enables you to organize your calendar, create and edit documents, calculate mortgage payments, and even send e-mails. They can be great devices if you are committed to learning and using them. However, for most real estate agents, I would consider these purchases as less than necessary. For many people, it can be a full-time job just keeping your PDA up to date. Nonetheless, any successful agent will carry an organizer of some sort with him or her at all times—even if it's spiral bound.

Oh My!

Who knows what new devices will be introduced in the months following the publication of this book? Technology evolves so fast that it is hardly practical to assume this chapter can keep up. As a general barometer, consider these rules when evaluating any sort of technical tool.

How to Evaluate a Real Estate Tool

Cost. How much does it cost, and how much will it return to you? Certainly, it may be difficult to measure the return on a technology investment, but you can probably "ballpark" it. Remember not to go crazy with the latest and greatest tool unless you believe it will ultimately pay for itself by making you a better agent.

TIP

One rule of thumb I've found useful is to avoid buying anything until I can't get along without it. That prevents me from wasting money on unnecessary tools.

Ease of use. Don't pay for anything that you will never use. You know yourself better than anyone else; are you really going to spend time organizing a PDA? You may even find that some devices cost you more in terms of time training than they ultimately pay back.

Ability to endure. Be sure to consider how long you expect the tool to last in your arsenal. If the device is only going to be useful for a short time, is it really worth the initial capital expenditure?

Remember, at the end of the day *you* are at the core of being a good real estate agent. While we have talked about a number of tools that will help you along the way, it is the individual that makes the difference.

10
Selling Online

You list a home and what's the first thing you do?

If you're like most agents, you get that sign planted in the yard. We all know that the sign is the single most important factor in finding a buyer, right?

That certainly used to be the case. However, today by some estimates as many as 70 to 75 percent of all homebuyers *first* use the Internet to locate their next home. And this number is only expected to climb in the coming years. This means that three out of four buyers are shopping on the Web. Will they find your for-sale sign out there? If you're not advertising online, you're missing out.

TRAP

The Internet is not *replacing* traditional real estate agent functions but *complementing* them. There is no substitute for a competent agent who can inform buyers and sellers about the local area, facilitate and manage the transaction, organize open houses, coach throughout the process, and perform a host of other functions. Top real estate agents will not fear the Internet but rather learn how to embrace the technology.

No Excuses Allowed

"But I don't know anything about the Internet."

"No one will buy a house online."

"It takes more time than it's worth."

Do any of these sound familiar? The excuses for avoiding the Internet are as plentiful as reasons for procrastinating on a new diet. Let's take each of the above in turn.

"But I don't know anything about the Internet."

You do not need to know anything about HTML, XML, or the NFL to get started online! These days, setting up a real estate agent Web site is a piece of cake and can cost as little as under $100. There are several companies who specialize in this setup, and they can do so in a very short time. For those who are a little more ambitious, you can have a Web site built from scratch for a few more dollars.

"No one will buy a house online."

While I agree that no one *should* buy a home over the Internet, this isn't to say it hasn't been done (check out eBay). Nonetheless, I am not advocating *virtual* sales. Nothing can replace the buyer's visiting the home in person and walking down the street.

However, there are several things that a buyer can do on the Web that are nearly impossible on foot. For example, it is easy to get instant crime statistics for the neighborhood with a few clicks. Also, buyers can quickly navigate maps of the area to find the proximity of the house to local shopping and schools. These are only two examples of the types information now available to home buyers over the Internet.

The point is simple: While people may not actually buy the home online, they are certainly using the Internet to research the home in terms of elements that will influence their decision to buy.

"It takes more time than it's worth."

For illustrative purposes, let's go back to our earlier example and follow the for-sale yard sign around for a month. It starts in your garage, where it owns a piece of space that could probably be better occupied. Then, it makes the giant leap to the trunk of your car, where it is sped around town. Then, finally it's planted in the lawn of your new listing. How much time do you think you spent planting that sign (or paying someone else to do it)?

Fifteen minutes, half an hour, one hour? Now consider that you need to plant signs in front of every home you list. Quickly we can see that the for-sale sign occupies a not insignificant amount of time in the long run.

Now consider the statistic saying that three-quarters of those hunting for homes *first* check the Internet. This suggests that the proportion of home buyers who find their property (if not their real estate agent) both from a yard sign and from the Internet is huge. This figure suggests that the two have equally important outcomes, but they most definitely do not have equal inputs.

The difference is that the bulk of effort and time that goes into your Web site is front-loaded. You will set up the Web site once, and then it runs in the background with little or no effort from you. It literally takes just a few minutes to input a new listing. Then potential buyers (and sellers) using a computer anywhere in the world can instantly find your portfolio of homes for sale.

Setting Your Sites

Your Web site will be the center of your online presence. It will serve as a complement to everything else you are doing to move your properties and also as a business card for selling yourself.

There are several different options for creating your own Web site; it's important that you choose one that fits your needs and personality. (Yes, Web sites have personalities!) The first decision you need to make is how much you are willing to invest in the Web site.

TIP

A Web site is definitely an investment. While you should not plan on dumping a ton of money in a site that will never get huge returns, there is a minimum level of Web presence that is considered necessary these days. Have anything less, and you are selling yourself short.

The pie chart in Figure 10.1 gives us a starting point at which to think about our technology budget. Remember that this not only represents Web site costs but also other technology gadgets. With almost every real estate agent packing a mobile phone and personal computer, these items cannot be ignored.

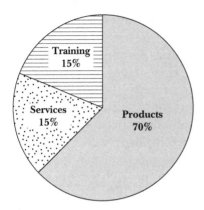

Figure 10.1 How to spend your technology budget.

Roughly speaking, based on expenditures from other industries, agents should spend around 30 percent on both training and services, while around 70 percent of total technology expenditures should be on products. Of course, these proportions are liable to change, depending on a number of different factors. For example, you may spend less on training if you already feel quite confident in the technology you are using or you may spend more on capital expenditures if you are just starting your career.

As a general rule, I do not advise beginning agents go crazy on technology spending. There are several reasons for this. First, many real estate agents simply cannot afford huge outlays of cash when getting started. Second, a basic Web site suffices for most beginning real estate agents. Third, the simple truth is that many real estate agents do not last long in the industry. With such a high turnover, minimal investment is wise until you have demonstrated to yourself (and your pocketbook) that greater investment in technology is wise.

This chart represents a few technologies plotted against cost and experience (that is, time as a real estate agent). By starting at the lower left-hand corner, we can see that the cell phone is the first and can be the most inexpensive technology gadget in which a beginning real estate agent should invest. Next, is the personal computer, which is likely to be among the most expensive purchases. The Web site is in the middle of both axes but extends to the upper end of cost as time spent as an agent grows. In other words, you should get a basic Web site early in your career as an agent and consider spending more money to update your Web presence over time.

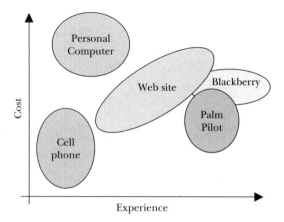

Figure 10.2 Prioritize your technology investments.

Depending on your needs (remember, cost and tenure are factors), you have several different options available that you can choose to set up your Web site. Generally speaking, there are three categories of Web sites:

1. Company Web sites
2. Templates from Web developers
3. Web site from scratch

Company Web Sites

Depending on where you are starting your career, there will likely be a Web site for the office. This Web site is important because it not only will attract potential buyers and sellers but also will send a signal to other agents. A good site signals a professional, well-oiled firm, while a poor site can really deter from a firm's image.

Within the office Web site, there is likely a list of agents, which many times will include headshots. This is the most basic Web presence you can have as an agent. It is essentially a yellow page listing—an online one.

Taking the company's Web site one step further, many brokerage companies will have pages within the company's Web site devoted to each agent in the office. Many offices will require agents to set up a page in their first days on the job and demand that these follow certain standards in presentation and verbiage.

Some of the larger offices will add a bunch of built-in features to their packaged agent sites. For example, you may be able to offer general real estate information, monthly mortgage calculators, and even listings directly through your company Web page. The more advanced Web sites will even pipe leads directly to your Web page from other sites. (We will talk more about online lead generation later in this chapter.)

The depth and breadth of the Web site you can create using your broker's template varies dramatically from office to office. Whether or not you also want to pursue other online offerings is up to you, depending on your circumstances. In my opinion, it never hurts to at least know your options.

TIP

Do not be afraid to embrace technology even more than others in your office. Many people let fear limit their reach online. The Web has drastically expanded the savvy real estate agent's potential. Do not let others intimidate you.

Templates from Web Developers

With the real estate boom of the last few years capturing so many people's attention, it's no surprise that a ton of businesses have popped up to cater to real estate agent's online needs. There are now dozens of companies that specialize in creating Web sites exclusively for real estate agents. These firms will use their templates to crank out a "custom" looking Web site in next to no time for you.

The advantage of these templates is cost and speed. They are usually far less expensive than building a Web site from scratch, unless you are comfortable with Internet technologies. They can be whipped up in as little as a few hours. The disadvantage is that one template looks very much like another.

Pricing Web site development can become tricky, as there are often at least two different components. The first is the initial Web site setup fees. This usually includes access to their templates (from which you can usually choose several different options), some basic text, a few pictures, and a few other bells and whistles. In addition to the setup fee is often the monthly cost of maintaining the Web site. This can be the most profitable component for the hosting company, as they usually charge you much more than it costs them to host your Web site. (They can do this because they've "hooked" you and know that you have a high switching cost.) There can be many other fees beyond the initial setup fee and monthly fee, so you should be vigilant when it comes to committing to a Web site developer.

TRAP

"Switching costs" is an economic term that is used to describe the cost a person feels when switching from one option to another. Say that you pay an initial $100 and spend two hours setting up your Web site. After this is all said and done, you find out that the company wants to charge you an additional $30 per month to maintain the Web site. You quickly learn that you can get another company to charge only $25 per month for the same services. Should you switch to the second, cheaper company? The answer is likely "no." The problem is that you have already invested the $100 and the time in the first company. It may ultimately cost you more money to start from scratch (even if you move to the cheaper option) because you would lose the initial $100 and the two hours you already spent. In a sense, you are "locked in" to the first option, and the switching costs are too high to justify jumping ship. Because of switching costs, it is important to choose your initial choice wisely. Be sure to look beyond a low initial cost and evaluate monthly or other hidden costs in your decision to join.

In addition to cost you will want to shop around among the Web developers to see how they compare on several other features. When looking, make sure you inquire about the following:

1. *Customer support.* You may have questions from time to time, and it is useful to know what you can expect from your Web provider. Some things to look for are Web site support, toll-free phone numbers, and online chat capabilities.

2. *Contract terms.* Make sure you know what you are getting into. Sometimes, Web developers try to lock you into a contract that is longer than you need. Know your options before you sign on the dotted line.

3. *Size of Web site.* Depending on the package you are buying, you may want to put up a number of pictures for houses you are trying to sell. In this event, you want to be sure you have enough space allocated for your needs.

4. *Privacy policy.* If you are like most of us, you probably rarely, if ever, read the privacy policy of Web sites you visit. However, doing so becomes increasingly important when you are looking to set up a professional relationship. The last thing you need is for a Web site to take and sell your personal information or to use it in a less-than-ethical manner. It may be well worth your time to read the company's privacy policy and ask questions about how they handle personal information.

5. *Features.* There are a ton of "add-on" features that you can include in your Web site. Not all may be suitable for your needs, but you should at least have an understanding of what you will need, and make sure the service you choose can accommodate it. (We will discuss the bells and whistles in greater detail later in this chapter.)

Web Site from Scratch

Building a Web site from scratch can be a daunting task. Even if you understand and are comfortable in the technology (few of us probably fall in this category), creating original and innovative content is not as easy as it sounds. Nonetheless, if you are up to the challenge, you can create a Web site with features that very few of your fellow agents will be able to match.

There are several steps to building a Web site from scratch. I recommend that you begin by writing down all of the features you want the site to have. This task is useful for two reasons. First, it will serve as a check to make sure that there really aren't cheaper and easier ways to build your site than starting from scratch. Second, it will help you organize and prioritize your needs.

Once you have successfully plotted the scope of your Web site, you have the choice to either build it yourself or hire a Web site developer to build off of your design. Much like building a house from scratch, there are people and companies that can aid you in each step of the process. While I will not go into the details of Web site design, I can generally suggest you consider the following when building from scratch:

1. *Domain name.* Although you may not know it, virtually every sensible Web site name has already been bought. Even though the site may not be developed, chances are someone owns the Web address, or universal resource locator (URL), also known as the domain name. Therefore, you must get creative when searching for a Web site name. I suggest you spend some time picking something that is meaningful to you personally, easy to remember, and easy to spell. To see if a particular domain is taken, check out www.networksolutions.com or www.godaddy.com. Both Web sites allow you to search for availability of a given Web name and, if available, enable you to buy it on the spot. Each company has different pricing schemes and different amenities, so make sure you pick the appropriate provider when it comes time to buy the domain name.

2. *Code.* There are several different ways to code a Web page. Some pages use frames to divide up different sections of the Web site. This is a quick and easy way to build a Web site, but it limits the ability of search engines to index the page. Therefore, most people prefer not to use frames in Web site design. Also, there are several different platforms and programming languages that people use. HyperText Markup Language, or HTML, is probably the most basic but many people use others such as Java, Extensible Markup Language (XML), Hypertext Preprocessor (PHP), ASP, NET, and a host of other technologies. If you're using a developer, make sure he or she knows the correct solution for your needs and builds a Web site with the most current and versatile technology.

3. *Browser compatibility.* It is estimated that over 90 percent of Web users rely on Microsoft's Internet Explorer to surf the Web. However, this percent has been dropping as users are defecting to Mozilla's Firefox browser as well as a host of others. While it probably won't make much difference in the near-term, you may want to save the time down the road by making sure your Web site is compatible with these other formats.

4. *Privacy.* If you are going to enable any sort of transmission of personal information, make sure you are using secure technology. This can be achieved relatively easy using Secure Socket Layer (SSL) technology.

5. *Information.* There is likely no point for a user to spend time surfing your site if it merely regurgitates what they already know. To start, share some personal information about yourself so that they can get a feel for who you are. Then, jump into your marketing pitch. Why should they spend more time with you or your Web site? Make sure there are plenty of links to other content within your Web site.

TIP

It is okay to use links to other, external Web sites on your own personal Web page. Surfers do not expect you to be the best at everything available on the Web, and they will be appreciative if you direct them to useful information—even if it's not on your Web site.

6. *Pictures.* One of the greatest assets you can provide on your Web site is pictures. These will likely include photos of properties you are listing, but they should also include a personal picture or two. You will want to make sure people can put a human face to the Web site so that you can win their trust. The more pictures the better, but remember, pictures cost bandwidth. In other words, the more pictures you have on the site, the slower it will run. Web users have a short attention span and will rarely wait a long time for your page to load. Be conscious of the performance of your site and work to find the right equilibrium of pictures and speed.

7. *Virtual tours.* A very neat extension of pictures that many real estate Web sites are now offering are virtual tours. These are video snippets of the house for sale. The video may include bits of the exterior of the house or various rooms inside. Depending on the technology, the user may be able to perform real-time edits to the video like zoom in or control the direction and speed of the image. Historically, this technology has been reserved for higher-end real estate listings, but increasingly more often we are seeing virtual tours being used for more modestly priced homes. Check out www.ipix.com.

8. *Local information.* You will want to add as much value as possible to your target audience. One way to do so is include information relevant to the local community. Try things like a local calendar of events or list of good restaurants in the neighborhood.

9. *Statistics.* People love statistics and often give the numbers more weight than they really deserve. Beef your Web site with information about local school districts, crime stats, median income level, or any other information that will give the user something interesting and relevant to take away from your Web site.

10. *Advertising.* This can be a give-and-take Web site attribute. You may want to advertise your Web site to attract users and, if you are fortunate enough to attract enough visitors, you may want to charge people to advertise on your Web site. The latter is a more difficult proposition, as there are so many Web sites available on the Web and so few that are actually able to generate any sizable amount of advertising revenue. Remember, we're not trying to compete with Google and Yahoo!

TIP

"Virtual curb appeal" is crucial. Just as the curb appeal of a house is very important (that is, the impression the house makes when you pull up to the curb), the same can be said for your Web site. Make sure your Web site makes an instant first impression. It should be aesthetically pleasing and easy to navigate.

Building Traffic on the Information Highway

Now that you've got a great-looking Web site, how are you going to attract users? After all, what good is a virtual road sign if no one is looking?

Traffic is the crux of most online businesses, and your Web site is no different. While your Web site does not depend on the millions of users that drive profits at many popular online sites, you do need a basal level of users.

Here are a few tips that will help you drive traffic and make your online presence known.

Search Optimization

Most people rely on search engines like Google and Yahoo! to organize the Web. Therefore, it is extremely important to be high in the results for searches on these Web sites. The keys to succeeding in the search engines vary from site to site and can be very complicated. However, here are a few tricks to help your site perform well.

- Many search engines rely on text within your Web site to figure out when and where to display it in the results. Therefore, use as much plaintext as possible without cluttering the Web site. Also, make sure to use sensible keywords that are specific to your particular niche (for example, use local landmarks or regional terms).

- Where possible, get others to link to your site. Google and other search engines rank sites' popularity, in part, based on how many other sites reference them. The idea is that if a reputable Web site is linking to yours, it lends credibility and therefore endorses the Web site.

- Metatags can be useful to help the search engine display appropriate text when your Web site is retrieved in the search results. These tags include a brief title and subject of your Web site. These are not required but can often make the textual representation of your Web site in a search engine more attractive to searchers.

- Most search engines do not require you to register or list your Web site with their engines. Instead, they rely on "spiders," which crawl through the Web and index the billions of Web pages available. However, you can submit your domain name to the search engines to guarantee it is checked. Also, some smaller and newer search engines may not immediately find your Web site unless it is explicitly entered. (These are probably not as important as the big players like Google and Yahoo!, though.)

Local Relevancy

Your Web site is likely filling a very particular niche. You should try to limit the relevancy of your Web site. Instead of providing general buying and selling information on your site, write a story with local relevancy. Has there been something new that is causing disruption in the local market? Perhaps you can create a calendar of local events that may be interesting to your target audience.

1. *Advertise your Web site.* You will definitely want to promote your Web site wherever possible. This means that the Web address

should be printed on all of your business cards. Also, make sure the domain is prominent on any flyers you send around. If you have invested in a good Web site, you want as many people to know about it as possible.

TIP

Most businesses operate via multiple channels. For example, Wal-Mart sells in their stores and on their Web site. Similarly, you will sell your houses via flyers, in personal conversations, and through your Web site. Make sure that you have a consistent channel strategy. Channel strategy simply implies that you are making an effort to have a consistent message in all your channels. Ensure that you have the same sale prices listed (if, for example, a seller cuts the price) on your flyers as on your Web site. Your phone number and personal contact information should be current in all places. In general, you want all of your sales channels to be current with the most consistent and accurate information.

2. *Listing in directories.* There are a few real estate agent directories available online. These directories will add your site to an index of other agent sites. This can be useful, as the combined catalog of sites may potentially generate more traffic than each site individually. (This phenomenon is referred to as "synergy," where the sum of the parts is greater than the individual components.) However, be wary of directories that charge a fee; make sure you are investing your money wisely.

3. *Reciprocal arrangements.* You are not alone in the online real estate world. However, just because there will be plenty of other real estate agents on the Web does not mean you are *all* working in competition. For example, an agent with a farm in the Los Angeles area is hardly competing with a similar agent working in San Francisco. In fact, these two agents might have something to offer each other. It is quite likely that someone from Los Angeles may be moving to San Francisco and therefore searching for a local agent—and vice versa. In situations like this, it may be very worth your while to seek out a partnership with an agent in a non-competing region. You can offer to exchange leads in a referral

arrangement. (Your office may already have such arrangements in effect.) In the rare circumstances in which you are creating a large amount of leads, you can even sell these leads to interested agents.

Leads, Leads, and More Leads

We have and will discuss how to grow and nurture leads in the real world, but now let's look at leads from cyberspace. Several new businesses are making tons of money buying and selling real estate leads over the Web. Depending on your circumstances, this may be a great opportunity.

The method by which companies capture the information of potential buyers and sellers varies drastically. Many provide free tidbits of information in exchange for the personal details of the curious user. This information is then sold to real estate agents for a fee.

TRAP

Many sites are transparent in their use and sale of personal information, but this is not true of all Web sites. Make sure you understand the business model of any Web site before you engage in a business transaction. If they are being deceitful or engaging in illegal activity, you definitely want to steer clear.

When Buying Leads

Here are a few things to consider when evaluating your decision to buy leads from an online vendor:

- *Cost.* The cost of these leads varies dramatically from company to company. I suggest you search around and discover what the going rate is per lead.

- *Quality of lead.* Companies will boast of having "high-quality" leads, but what does this really mean? Make sure the company is selling you current, correct information of people who are interested in buying and selling property *and* are interested in being contacted by an agent such as yourself.

- *Relevance of lead.* It doesn't do any good for the real estate agent in Omaha to buy a lead for someone looking to buy in Honolulu. Make sure the leads you are considering buying are relevant to you.

- *Minimum lead generation.* Are you guaranteed a minimum number of leads? Some sites will require you to pay regardless of the number of leads generated. This could leave you dry, if they are unable to get enough relevant leads.

- *Marketing features.* Some Web sites offer a number of services in addition to just selling the leads. These companies may have things like automatic e-mail with your contact information, routine updates for buyers who are on a longer time horizon, or other online resources available to help convert the lead to a sale. Make sure you know what other services, if any, your lead generator offers.

Pulling Sales from Your Web Site

Once you navigate through the Web of offerings and establish an online presence, it's time to seal the deal. Now you must convert the leads and nibbles that will come through your Web site into actual transactions. Doing so can be easier said than done, but it is not impossible.

The first thing to remember is that the Web and traditional mediums are not in opposition but rather work in concert. Once you are able to get a lead from your Web site (or another), follow up with that person in some form. You can easily reach him or her through an e-mail message. However, you can often make more of an impact by calling the person directly. (Remember from your own experience how easy it is to delete a random e-mail message and how hard it is to ignore a personal phone call?)

TIP

Having several e-mail "templates" and voicemail "talking points" ready for follow-up with a potential client is sometimes helpful. Since many of these leads will result in nothing more than having spent a few minutes with others, be sure to be as efficient as possible. Create talking points and templates that can easily be modified as much as possible based on what you know about the lead. In this manner, you can minimize the effort you spend with correspondence in the early stages of converting a lead.

TRAP

By ignoring the specific needs of your clients, you may alienate them. Be sure that, if you use a template or talking points to correspond with a potential buyer or seller, you are customizing the message enough to suit her or his specific needs. You won't win any friends by sending an open house notice to someone not interested in moving for another six months.

Try Handwriting

Another way to make an impression on a potential client is by sending a handwritten letter. As odd as this may sound, it can have great results. I recently spoke with a top-performing real estate agent who told me that her best results in corresponding with cold leads is a handwritten invitation to discuss their needs. From her experience, people are overwhelmed with the effort and personal attention. Again, remember how easy it can be to intertwine cutting-edge technology (for example, a lead from your Web site) with old-school human touches (for example, handwritten note).

Help Is a Few Clicks Away

To learn more about agent Web sites and to find other tips and traps for selling online, visit www.RobertIrwin.com/AgentsCorner.aspx .

11

Getting Buyers and Sellers to Sign

Making the deal is part art, part science, and part luck. All successful real estate agents have perfected their own techniques for getting it done. And until you, as a new agent, perfect yours and are able to make deals, you won't graduate into their ranks.

In this chapter we're going to examine real estate negotiating. We'll see what's required to get buyers and sellers to agree to the same terms on a purchase agreement.

The Basics

As agents know, in order to make a deal in real estate, all the terms, including price and financing, must be in writing.

TRAP

According to the statute of frauds adopted in all states, transactions for the purchase and sale of real estate must be in writing.

Both parties, buyer and seller, must sign the same agreement. If there is even the slightest difference in the terms between what buyer and seller signs, then there is no deal. Let's talk about some nuances here.

You are representing a buyer who wants to purchase a home with an asking price of $250,000. Your buyer makes an offer of $225,000. (We won't worry about financing for now.)

You present this offer to the seller, who doesn't like it because it's so much lower than the asking price. But the seller is desperate and so agrees. However, just before signing, the seller says, "I've got to have $500 more." So, he crosses out the price and changes it to $225,500. Then he signs. Have you got a deal?

Nope. Not unless you take it back and the buyers agree to the $500 increase, which they very well might. Only when they sign the same document with the same price as the seller signed have you got a deal.

Let's try again. Same deal, only this time the seller agrees to the price, exactly. Only he adds a clause saying that the entrance hall chandelier is not part of the sale; he plans to take it with him. Have you got a deal?

Nope. Not unless the buyers agree to the new terms, which they very well might not, if they cherish that chandelier as well. (Many a deal has been lost over a piece of personal property.)

The basics are that everything has to be in writing. And both buyers and sellers have to agree to exactly the same purchase agreement by signing.

Getting Buyers to the Dotted Line

Sometimes you'll show a home to buyers and they'll fall in love with it. Everything will be perfect, and they'll ask you to please take their offer to the seller, which will be for cash, full price, no contingencies. Does that happen often? I think not, but every experienced agent can usually recall it happening once or twice during a lifetime.

A much more common occurrence is when the buyers aren't quite sure about the home, they are afraid to make an offer, they want to lowball the seller, and getting adequate financing is a problem. That's what more commonly happens and is when salesmanship comes into play. Let's break it down piece by piece.

The Buyers Aren't Sure About the Property

Every good salesperson knows that you aren't going to get a deal until you find a property that a purchaser wants to buy. However, many times the property isn't going to be perfect; it's going to be a compromise. You may have taken the buyers out half a dozen times and they've seen every home in their price range in the area. They aren't really happy with any of them. But, they want and need a home, now.

So you talk to them about the homes they've seen and, between you and them, you come up with five of the best choices. And you take them back to see those five houses. Now you're sitting around a table as they try to decide which, if any, they want to buy.

TRAP

Sometimes going back to the office is a mistake. When you're at the home that buyers like, it may be a good idea to start writing up their offer right there, or even in the car, if the sellers are home and you can't do it in the house. Strike while the iron is hot, so to speak.

It's important to understand your role as an agent. It's your fiduciary duty to do the best for your client. That does not include talking them into a house that they don't want. But it does include giving them enough information to make an intelligent choice on a house that they may want.

Giving them information includes all the data about the houses they are considering. It may include asking them what they like about the houses and then what they dislike. Once you know what they like and dislike, you may want to bring out information that they hadn't considered before, which could help them decide.

For example, they may dislike the fact that the house they are considering only has three bedrooms, and they want four. You may point out that a four-bedroom house is available to them, but it's not the floor plan they want, and it's higher than they can afford to pay. You may ask if they're quite sure they can't get by with three bedrooms. Many people do. Sometimes it's not necessary to have a guest room, for example, since it simply stays vacant 95 percent of the time. Might not one of the other bedrooms double as an office and a guest room? Could two of the kids double up when there's company?

TIP

Where there's a will, there's a way. Often there can be work-arounds when objections are examined more closely.

It may very well be that the buyers simply haven't considered all of the possibilities in a compromise and once they do so, the house they are iffy about will turn into a solid choice. It's up to you to take the objections that buyers raise and examine them closely. Is there a realistic way around? Will it satisfy their needs and desires?

TRAP

Remember, it's most unlikely that your buyers will find the "perfect" house. It's much more likely that every house they see will be at least a bit wrong. Nearly every home purchase is a compromise in some way or another.

Here are some common objections to the less than perfect house and potential work-arounds:

Possible Objections to the Property and Work-Arounds

The Price Is Too High

- Is it really too high for the market, or does it just seem high to the buyers? Look at comparable houses.

- Can they afford it, if it turns out not to be overpriced? Check the financing.

- Do the buyers want to make an offer at a lower price that they consider right?

The Floor Plan Is Wrong

- Sometimes floor plans can be rearranged by moving walls and doors. Will the buyers consider this?

- Awkward floor plans are often a matter of perception. Go back to the house and study it again.

- Can the buyers live with the floor plan, if the price is right? Consider a lower-than-asking-price offer.

The House Needs Paint and Cleaning

- Will the buyers consider it if the sellers will fix it up or provide an allowance for fix-up? Add such a contingency to an offer.

- Will the buyers consider it as fixer-upper, buy as-is for a lower price, and do the work themselves? Make a lower-than-asking-price offer.

The House Is Too Big or Too Small

- Have the buyers really analyzed how much room they actually need? Consider a room-by-room estimate of living space.

- Can the buyers realistically afford a larger house in this market? Tour some bigger homes that may cost more.

- Are there features that the buyers like in this house that outweigh those they don't want? Make a list and compare feature-by-feature.

The Property Is in the Wrong School District

- Have the buyers seen any homes they could afford in the "right" school district? Explain that school districts affect price.

- Will they consider a smaller, less expensive house to get the school district they want? Show them condos, townhouses, and smaller homes.

- Will they consider a "second-best" school district? Get test scores from both districts and compare.

The Neighborhood Is Run-Down

- Is it really, or are just a few houses? All neighborhoods tend to have a few bad apples. Tour the area again to see.

- Do the buyers feel the neighborhood might change? Are there other new buyers fixing up homes? Is there a home owner's association that's working hard to clean up the area? Ask if your buyers are willing to get out there and help make changes.

- Does the price warrant the area? Perhaps the buyers should reconsider what houses cost, how much of a house they want, and where they want it.

The Buyers Want to Lowball the Sellers

Sometimes buyers will decide that this is, in fact, the property for them. No, it may not be perfect, but it's good enough that they'll compromise on it and they want to make an offer.

No, don't spend your commission just yet. You're still at the start of negotiations and not the end. The buyers want to make an offer, but they want to lowball it—offer substantially less than the sellers are asking.

Many agents hate to take in lowball offers. They just know that the sellers aren't going to accept them. Further, the sellers may get angry, as may the listing agent, for wasting their time. And even if the sellers are willing to listen, it is very likely they'll counteroffer, sometimes at very close to their asking price, which the buyers may now reject.

TRAP

Don't refuse to take lowball offers. Consider the lowball offer an education for all concerned, particularly the buyers. Besides, you never know what the sellers might accept.

As an agent who presumably knows the market and the value of the home, you may realize that a lowball offer doesn't have a chance of being accepted. You feel it is a disservice to your buyers, not to mention the sellers and other agents, to take one. So what do you do?

When the Buyers Want to Lowball the Sellers

Make sure the buyers understand current market values.

- Part of your job is education. Perhaps you haven't done it very well. Show the buyers the selling prices of recent comps. If necessary, tour other houses in the same price range.
- Explain market trends. Show the buyer's published reports, inventories, time it takes to sell, and so on that explain which way the market is heading.

- Examine how long the house has been for sale. Point out that homes on the market for a very short time are unlikely to command a much lower price, as sellers are still optimistic about getting close to full price. Explain that homes on the market a very long time are more likely to be sold for less because the sellers may be more willing to consider any offer, even lowball ones. Show the buyers the difference between "list" and "sales" prices on recent deals, which are usually available from the MLS.

Find out if the buyers are looking to "steal" a house.

- Some buyers, usually investors, only want to buy *if* they can get a "steal" on the price. They may be willing to have you take in 20 or 30 lowball offers on the hope that one will get accepted. If you're willing to work with this kind of buyer, fine. If not, perhaps you should ask them to work with a different agent.

- Do the buyers understand the value of real estate? A few buyers simply think they can make any offer, 10, 20, or even 40 percent off asking price and have a realistic chance of having it accepted. Explain that sellers may owe so much on their property that they can't sell for much less than asking price. Or that the market's so hot that most sellers won't even consider it.

Make sure the buyers understand how negotiating works,

- If the buyers really like the house, explain that making a lowball offer might end up costing them more later on. The sellers might simply reject the lowball offer out of hand. In such a case, the buyers might have to come back and offer much more to entice the sellers to the negotiating table, and perhaps they would end up paying more than if they had made a reasonable offer at the beginning.

The Buyers Say They Want the House, but Don't Have Enough Cash

In today's market it's often the case that buyers have more cash available than they realize. The reason is that financing has been revolutionized to the point where nothing down, even nothing down and no closing costs, have become commonplace.

When the buyers say they don't have enough cash, try to determine just how much cash they have—and how much they realistically need after securing a mortgage.

TIP

When it comes to financing, buyers may be hesitant to discuss their personal finances with you. Therefore, it's often a good idea to suggest they contact a good mortgage broker. He or she can usually provide a letter of pre-approval that will state the maximum loan they can afford, or the maximum monthly payment at a given interest rate, or both. From this information you should be able to deduce quickly how much they can afford to pay for a property. Keep in mind that cash and financing go hand in hand. When there's less of one, you need more of the other.

TRAP

Determine what buyers can afford based on their financing abilities and cash availability as early in the house-hunting process as possible. This way, you can show them homes that are within their grasp, rather than wasting time for both of you on homes that are out of reach.

It's often the case that the real reason buyers "don't have the cash" to buy a house they've seen and like is because the agent hasn't properly qualified them and has shown them properties that are unrealistic given their price range. If this happens, it's time to start over. Qualify the buyers ... and show them what they can realistically afford.

Find Out If They Can Raise More Cash

Sometimes buyers don't really know how much cash they have available, if they really need it. The following are some other sources of cash that you can suggest when the buyers come up short.

Other Sources of Cash

- Certificates of Deposit (CDs), Individual Retirement Accounts (IRAs), and other penalty accounts. Perhaps to the buyers it's worth paying the penalty and taxes to get the house.

- Other assets against which buyers can borrow to get cash. These could include a stock portfolio, coin collection, a locked-in bank account, and so on.

- Another property buyers can refinance or sell.

- Personal property such as a motor home, boat, antique furniture, and so on that could be sold to raise cash.

- Any other asset that could be conveniently converted to cash (or even traded to the seller) to facilitate making the deal.

SPECIAL CAUTION

Never suggest that buyers use money to purchase a home that they might otherwise need for living expenses, retirement, or other necessary needs. Have them check with their accountant to see just what they can realistically afford to cash in to buy a house.

The Buyers' Credit Is a Problem

You should learn whether the buyers' credit is a problem either directly from the buyers or from a mortgage broker when they attempt to get a pre-approval letter. If there is a problem, ask the buyers if they can work it out with the mortgage broker. Often going to a different lender, paying a higher interest rate, or getting a different kind of mortgage can solve the problem.

TRAP

Usually a credit problem manifests itself in the form of a credit report that produces a low credit score. Don't tell your buyers that a low score can be "fixed." It usually can't. Over time they may be able to raise their score dramatically *if* they maintain good credit. And if mistakes were made on the credit report, correcting these can also produce a turnaround. However, other than these two remedies, most others won't work and may waste the buyer's money.

If the problem proves intractable, then you may need to explain to the buyers that they may not be able to get financing on a house at this time. You may want to suggest other alternatives:

Alternatives When Buyer's Credit Is a Problem

- Have the buyer put up lots of cash and get an asset mortgage. In this situation the institutional lender usually wants 30 percent or more down and uses the value of the property (the asset) as the basis of the financing. The buyer normally doesn't have to satisfy any credit requirements. (Indeed, the lender actually hopes the buyer will default on the mortgage so it can take back the property at a profit!)

- Get the seller to finance the buyer. Some sellers want (or at least are willing) to give "paper" to buyers in order to get an interest rate higher than they can get in the bank or just to sell the property. Be sure that the sellers fully understand, in writing, what the buyer's true credit status is so that they don't come back later on to accuse you of pulling a fast one on them. (This usually happens only if the buyer eventually defaults on the seller's mortgage.)

- Get a subprime loan. Institutional lenders today will offer a mortgage to almost anyone if the interest rate is high enough. It might cost the buyers as much as twice the market rate, and they might have to put 10 to 20 percent down, but chances are that some lender somewhere will give them a loan. Get a good mortgage broker who specializes in subprime financing.

TIP

"Subprime" means lending to borrowers who don't qualify for a "conforming" mortgage, or one that passes the underwriting standards of Fannie Mae and Freddie Mac. These are the two large secondary lenders that set the standards for the best loans available in real estate.

The Buyers Are Afraid to Make the Move

It's often been said, but bears repeating, that buying a house is usually the biggest single financial transaction a person makes in his or her lifetime. Is it any wonder that many buyers get "cold feet" when it's time to buy?

The buyers may want the house, even desperately. They have the cash and the financing, yet they won't commit to a purchase agreement. It may now be time for you to do some hand holding.

You may want to simply bring the issue out into the open. "What is it that's holding you back?" "What are your fears?" "What's the worst that can happen?"

The buyers may protest that they don't really have any fears, except that the price is huge . . . and so are the monthly payments.

You can point out that, yes, the price of the home may be a quarter million dollars, or even a million, but compared to other homes, it's not unusual. Further, that unless the market rapidly deteriorates, the value is likely to be there. Over time, they may be able to refinance to get money out, if needed, and eventually sell, probably for a profit. So, although it's a huge amount of money, it's not like throwing it away.

You can also point out that high payments are like the "sticker shock" that new car buyers sometimes face. Yes, the payments may be high, but assuming the financing is reasonable, they should be able to handle it. Certainly the finance company thinks so.

Finally, you can simply point out that sometimes in our lives we have to take a chance, make a leap of faith. Maybe this is one of those times for the buyers.

Sooner or later your buyers will take a deep breath and make the leap—they'll sign. Or not! (Sometimes would-be buyers simply can't handle the pressure and back out.) Either way, you'll soon know for certain where you stand in terms of making the deal.

Protecting Yourself and Your Client

Finally, a word about an important function you perform as an agent. Part of the reason many people will come to you, in many cases the larger part, is because of the expertise you offer. They're paying you a commission because they trust you to know the ropes, to be able to avoid the costly entanglements and pitfalls that await the unwary.

TIP

Always remember that much of what you do for your buyers, they can do for themselves, including making an offer, getting financing, and closing a deal. A big part of what you bring to the table is protection. You're protecting them against making a costly mistake, protecting them from the other party, indeed, even protecting them from doing something stupid by themselves.

You are morally, ethically, and, in some cases, legally bound to protect your buyer/seller. Mess up and there could be all Hell to pay!

All of which is to say, that even going beyond what you learn when you got your license, you should take the time to educate yourself as to the laws of your state, community, and those federal laws that apply, regarding real estate. Learn all about inspection reports, disclaimers, disclosures, contracts, and more. And remember that, presumably, you're not a lawyer—so refer all legal matters to an attorney.

Be the best agent you can be for your clients. And you can be sure that they will amply reward you.

12

Closing the Deal and Managing The Escrow

Many a new real estate agent feels that the work is done when both buyer and seller sign the purchase agreement on the dotted line. Experienced agents, however, know that very often that's just when the real work gets started.

It's a huge mistake to think that you've earned your commission just because you've got a deal. To earn that commission you must be able to walk that deal through an often torturous route to the close of escrow. As those in the field know, an *escrow* is a "stakeholder," usually a neutral attorney or a company. The escrow accepts all funds and paperwork needed to complete the transaction. When everything is in, the escrow is said to be "perfect." The escrow holder then records the deed in favor of the buyer and disperses all funds including those that go to the seller and agents.

In reality, you don't know if you're going to get your commission until that check is in your hand.

Working a Modern Real Estate Transaction

Not that many years ago, getting buyers and sellers to agree in writing meant a lot more than it does today. Then, most people felt it was a solid contract, virtually cast in stone. In today's world, however, a purchase agreement, in effect, is more like a letter of intent.

Perhaps the best way to think of a real estate transaction is in two parts. The first part occurs when both parties sign. The second part occurs after all of the contingencies have been removed. Only then can the deal move forward to its conclusion.

A MODERN REAL ESTATE TRANSACTION

PART 1: Buyers and Sellers Sign

PART 2: All Contingencies Are Removed and Escrow
    Can Proceed to Closure

The Agent's Job

Your job is twofold. First, you need to bring the buyer and the seller together. Second, you need to see that escrow is opened, that all of the contingencies are removed, and that escrow closes.

TIP

In today's real estate, the agent may represent the seller, the buyer, or both, as in a dual agency. Be sure you understand the ramifications of each of these relationships and that you declare whom you represent clearly to your client in writing. Remember, who pays the commission has no bearing on whom you represent.

While you're likely to be mostly on your own with regard to the first part, many offices offer help with the second. Your broker or manager may help with the closing of escrow, or there may be a special "closer" in your office who does this. Regardless, if it's your deal, it's up to you to see that everything moves along.

In all of the other chapters in the book we're dealing with how to get to a deal, in essence how to get the first part done. In this chapter we're going to concentrate on how to close a deal, the second part.

Handling Negotiations

Bringing the buyer and seller together for the initial deal involves drawing up the purchase document and getting agreement by both parties. Typically it will involve offer and counteroffer until a deal is made. Today, a standard part of this deal will be a number of contingencies that usually include the following:

Typical Contingencies Found in a Purchase Agreement

- *Financing.* The buyer must qualify for an appropriate mortgage, or else the deal is off.

- *Inspection.* The buyer must approve a professional inspection of the home.

- *Disclosures.* The buyer must approve the seller's disclosures of any existing defects in the home.

- *Sale of current home.* There is no deal until the buyer can sell her or his existing house.

- *Other contingencies.* Any other contingency written into the offer.

Almost all of these contingencies are limited by time. For example, the buyers typically may have 30 days to remove the financing contingency, 14 days to approve the inspections, 3 days to approve the disclosures, and 45 to 60 days to dispose of their current home. If at any time the buyers do not remove these contingencies (or, if it's a seller's contingency, the seller does not remove it), the sale is off.

What this means is that very often, there will be a renegotiation of the deal within a few weeks after it was initially signed. Let's consider an example.

Renegotiation Based on a Professional Inspection

The buyers pay for a professional inspector to look at the home. The inspector goes through and discovers that the roof leaks. The recommendation is that it be replaced.

If you're representing the buyers, they may insist that the sellers pay for a new roof. They are adamant, so you format the demand in terms of a renegotiation. The buyers will continue with the deal *if* the sellers pay for the roof.

If you're representing the sellers, now you have to show them why they need to pay for a roof replacement (which could easily cost $15,000 or more), come up with a counteroffer, or forget the deal. They don't want to pay for a new roof, saying they've only owned the home three years themselves. Why should they be responsible for 25 years of wear and tear?

You may argue that the roof really is in bad shape and needs to be repaired, and if they're going to sell the house, to these buyers or to any others, it will have to be dealt with. However, a less costly alternative may be to patch the roof rather than replace it. They jump at that idea, so you present a counteroffer saying the sellers will patch but not replace the roof.

If you represent the buyers, you may recommend that a good roofer examine the property to determine if patching is possible. The roofer says, no, it needs to be replaced. But you know that the sellers won't pay for a whole new roof. So you ask the buyers if they'll compromise. Will they accept a credit on the purchase price of half the cost of a new roof? If they accept, the contingency can be removed and the deal moves forward. If not, more negotiation may be necessary, or the deal might be lost.

TRAP

All contingencies must be removed *in writing* for everyone's protection.

Renegotiation Based on Other Contingencies

Similarly, negotiations on the purchase may be reopened based on the sellers' disclosures. The sellers disclose that there's a crack in the foundation. The buyers refuse to purchase unless and until it's fixed. Who pays for it? When will it be done? These things need to be settled before the deal can move forward.

Or, the buyers discover that their lender won't fund. They need to get a new lender. But, time specified in the finance contingency in the purchase agreement has run out for them; there's no time left to get appropriate financing. So, the buyers can ask for more time. But, the sellers can back out of the deal. It's renegotiation time, and you're it when it comes to saving the deal.

The same can happen when time runs out for the buyers to sell their old home or any other contingency expires. It can be like starting all over again.

The Agent's Role in Removing Contingencies

As we've seen, contingencies can make or break a deal. What should also be apparent is that normally they have a time frame and usually there's an opportunity to renegotiate.

TRAP

When a contingency runs out, the affected party potentially can simply say "no" and back out of the deal. This usually doesn't happen, however, because in most cases both parties still want the deal to move forward.

Thus, in addition to all your other chores involving working with other buyers and sellers, prospecting, farming, and so on, you have to shepherd the deal along. *You* have to be mindful of deadlines and be sure they are met. *You* have to be on the spot to handle the renegotiations. This is why those experienced agents often say the real work doesn't start until the deal is signed.

Sometimes it's helpful to have a list of all the possible tasks that you may become involved in when you close a deal. The following list details many of them. Of course, in some offices a manager or other agent will handle some of them. Nevertheless, it's your deal, and it's up to you to see that everything moves along faultlessly. Let something drop through the cracks and your commission could go along with it.

Agent's Tasks in Closing the Escrow

Open Escrow. The buyer and seller should agree who will handle escrow. Sometimes your broker may insist that it be handled by your in-office escrow department. There may be conflicts of interest here, and federal rules may apply. Consult with your broker. You may open escrow, or another agent may do so.

TRAP

Time is of the essence in any real estate contract. Getting everything done in a timely fashion is essential. Normally, escrows have a time limit, say 30 or 45 days, to become perfect and close. If the time limit is not met, the deal may fall through.

Get Preliminary Escrow Instructions. These tell escrow how to per-form and are based on the purchase agreement. To protect your client, you should see that they are drawn properly. (More often than you may think, they are not.) If you're not sure, you may want your broker or office attorney to examine them.

Obtain Disclosures. If you represent the sellers, you may need to provide them with your office's approved disclosure forms. You will also need to provide a federal disclosure with regard to lead and any other disclosures that are needed. As an agent of the buyer, you'll need to get these to the buyers to sign off or to begin renegotiations based on them.

Remove Contingencies. You should have a list of contingencies and when they time out. If you represent the buyers, what you will want to do includes the following:

- Obtain necessary financing.
- Arrange for a professional inspection and secure the buyers' approval.
- Obtain disclosures from the sellers and secure the buyers' approval.
- Be sure the sellers get a termite clearance, which is required for most financing, and be sure required work, usually paid for by the sellers, will be done.
- Fulfill all requirements to remove any other contingencies.

  If you represent the sellers you'll want to do this:

- Be sure they can give clear title.
- Arrange for a termite report and any other needed report and clearance, and see that necessary work is done.
- Follow up on buyers obtaining the necessary financing.
- Do whatever else is necessary to complete escrow.

TIP

As an agent, you need to be proactive. That means that not only must you do all the jobs necessary for your clients, but you must follow up to see that the other agent, assuming there is one, is doing everything necessary for the other party. In the final analysis, it doesn't matter who didn't do their job—finger pointing won't help. If something essential doesn't get done, you might not get a commission. So, you've got to see that it all comes together.

Follow Up on Documentation. The escrow officer will presumably prepare all documents necessary to close escrow, except the loan documents which will be produced by the finance company. You need to be sure everything is prepared correctly in a timely fashion. If there's something you don't know or don't understand, ask your broker/manager or the officer attorney.

TRAP

Don't rely on escrow officers! They won't do your job, and sometimes they won't even do all of theirs. You've got to constantly follow up to be sure that everything gets done in a timely fashion so the deal will close.

Follow Up on Repairs. As part of the renegotiations in terms of disclosures and inspections or as part of the conditions of the termite or other report, physical work on the property may be required. This must be done in a timely fashion for escrow to close. You have to be on top of this to be sure it gets done. Remember, Rome wasn't built in a day, and fixing a roof or repainting a home can't usually be done in a day, either. Get started early.

Contact Your Clients Regularly. Let them know how things are moving along, to keep them from worrying and possibly doing something to crash the deal. This will also allow you to determine if something new has affected them, such as a job layoff, which could prevent the buyers from qualifying for a mortgage.

Do Whatever Else Is Required. You can't afford to let the ball drop. You should check regularly with the escrow officer and be sure everything is being done in a timely fashion.

Handle a Final Inspection. This is usually done by buyers and their agent just prior to closing. It's not a time for reopening negotiations but rather to see that the property is essentially the same as when the deal was originally inked. Be sure the property is ready to be transferred (empty and clean). Work out any small problems with the other agent.

Get Final Instructions Signed. If you represent the buyers, this means getting them down to the escrow office to sign the loan documents. If you represent the sellers, it means getting them to sign the deed. And both parties must sign off the final escrow instructions.

TRAP

Remember, unless you're a lawyer, you can't give legal advice. If there's a legal problem with the escrow documents, get legal advice from an attorney to handle it.

Transfer Possession of the Property. If you represent the sellers, get the key to the buyer's agent and be sure your client gets their check. If you represent the buyers, present them with the keys to their new property.

TRAP

I always advise new buyers to get the locks changed. It's a safety precaution that helps protect them and the agent.

Your job as the agent is to handle both parts of the deal: finding the buyers or sellers and getting them to sign. And then closing. Until you've done both parts, you haven't finished the job. And you won't get that important commission check until that job is done.

13

Staging—To Be or Not to Be?

Over the last few years "staging" has become an important part of selling a home in many markets. However, it also has become quite controversial. Twenty years ago if you asked an agent if he or she "staged" listings, you would probably get a puzzled look. Today if you ask, you're likely to get an enthusiastic "absolutely!" or negative "never!"

Usually the reason for the vehemence behind the answer has to do with cost and, more important, who pays for it. We'll look into that shortly, but let's be sure we're all on the same page when it comes to staging: Just what is it?

What Is Staging a House?

In Real Estate 101, you were told that a house that shows well should sell faster and for more money than one that shows badly, all else being equal. In fact, agents will sometimes eliminate a house that shows badly from the list they plan to show their buyers, unless they categorize it as a "fixer."

TIP

A "fixer-upper," also known as a "handyman special," is a home that is in bad shape, shows badly, and usually has the price knocked down because of its condition.

Agents will normally tell their sellers, if the sellers don't ask first about it, to fix up and clean up their homes to get them ready for showing. Agents will "suggest" to sellers that, in order to get top dollar and a quicker sale, they should paint over marks on walls, clean the carpets, and in general tidy up the place.

The problem is that the vast majority of sellers simply don't know how to get their homes ready for sale. To most of them, it looks fine just the way it is. After all, they've been living in it since they bought it and it's comfortable for them. Why shouldn't it be fine for the next owner? This kind of resistance can be difficult to overcome.

One way of dealing with it is by asking sellers to take a few hours to visit the model homes of any nearby building development. Ask them to look at the colors, the flooring, the furniture, the arrangements, and the like. You can point out that these homes have been "staged" to sell. Special interior decorators have come in and put just the right amount and the right kind of furniture, coloring, and effects in the home to show it off. Staging makes a home look its best for buyers.

TRAP

Buyers have no imagination. It's important to make sellers understand that telling a buyer that "a bookshelf would look great here" or to "take away this couch and look at the extra space you'll have" are spoken on deaf ears. You have to put the bookshelf in place and remove the couch before buyers can "see."

Thus, staging amounts to physically preparing the house for sale—making it shine inside and out so that it will grab buyers and make them want to buy it.

Where Are Homes Staged?

In the past, staging was primarily done only for the most expensive homes. A special design team would come in and paint, recarpet, redo landscaping, put in rented furniture, and turn the home into a dollhouse, a shining showpiece. Since this treatment cost tens of thousands of dollars, it's easy to see why only the most costly homes received it.

Over the past decade, however, in places such as California, Florida, and New York City, agents selling more modest homes have begun staging them. Today, this practice has become increasingly common in all parts of the country.

But today's staging is often a far cry from what it was in the past, when only the most expensive homes were treated. Today, staging may mean nothing more than having a crew come out and mow and trim the landscaping; wash down the driveway; clean the carpets; wash the toilets, sinks, and tile work; and otherwise clean up. The cost may only be a few hundred dollars. But even just a basic staging can make an enormous difference in the appearance of the home and both its potential sales price and rapidity of finding a buyer.

Does Staging Really Pay?

The big question is whether staging really does pay, and it's part of the controversy. While common sense indicates that a staged home should sell faster and for more money than one that isn't, I haven't seen any reliable studies that have proven it. In fact, sometimes a staged home will simply sit on the market for months without selling. Of course, this often can be traced to a problem such as overpricing.

TIP

A properly staged home should bring a top-market price. But, it won't bring an above-market price. Remember, staging doesn't turn a Ford into a Mercedes; it just makes the Ford look the most presentable it can be.

Nevertheless, as an agent you should ask yourself, "What would I rather show?" Would it be a home in which everything is neat, clean, and good looking? Or would it be a home where there is clutter, dirt, and even squalor? Which would appeal more to your buyers?

When promoting property to other agents, in fact, one of the best things you can say is that it "shows well." What you're telling the other agent is that the property won't embarrass them. It won't turn their buyers off, not only against the property, but perhaps against the agent who they perceive as wasting their time by showing it.

Who Should Pay for It?

Now we come to the big question and the bigger reason for the controversy: Who should pay for the cost of staging?

Obviously, the sellers should pay for it, you may say. It's an improvement to their home. They benefit from, it is hoped, a higher price and quicker sale. End of argument, right?

Except that most sellers don't see it that way.

They keep looking at that big commission they are going to have to pay you and keep asking and telling themselves, "Why doesn't the agent pay for the staging? After all, what else is he or she doing to warrant receiving all that money? It should be part of the costs of doing business."

Whoa! At this point nearly every agent I know is going to point out that he or she only gets paid if the property sells. If they put up the money for staging and the property doesn't sell for whatever reason, they're out the funds. That's no way to run a business, certainly not a real estate business.

Further, with splits the way they are, few agents feel that they can really afford to stage a property. Even though the total commission may be large, your share of it probably isn't.

Finally, a new agent just getting started undoubtedly doesn't have the up-front money to stage a property. What with just scrimping to the first commission check, where are the extra bucks to come from to stage?

TRAP

 Some new agents borrow the money to stage a listing. While this works out well *if* the property sells and *if* there's an agreement for reimbursement with the seller, it doesn't work so well when those two "ifs" don't hit. My suggestion is that, as a beginning agent, you pass on it, if your broker or the seller won't pop for the staging, and try to get the sellers to do a better job of cleaning and fixing on their own.

Some industrious agents even will offer to come by one day and work hand to hand with the sellers to fix and clean up the property. This offer has two problems. The first is that neither the seller nor you may know what needs to be done (see below). The second is that instead of making the seller indebted to you, it can make the seller wonder just how professional you are: Why would a busy agent have time to come by to clean floors?

Another possible compromise is to get the sellers to agree to pay for the staging *if* the property sells. The agent will foot the bill initially and be paid back upon sale. For someone new in the business, you will probably have to run it past your broker/manager and get him or her to put up the initial funds. Some offices are okay with this arrangement, but many who haven't staged in the past will quickly turn it down. Then you're on your own.

TIP

Staging can cost as much or as little as you want to spend. A basic clean and run only costs about $250, but it can make a big difference in a dirty home. Add touch-up painting, rug cleaning, excess furniture removal and storage, and the price quickly goes up to $1,000. Add refurbishing the front yard, repainting the front of the house, and repainting and recarpeting parts of the interior, and $5,000 to $10,000 will go so quickly it'll make your head spin.

The Other Problem with Sellers

Assuming you can get the money to stage a property, you probably will have to deal with the seller's feelings. We've already mentioned that sellers may resist any suggestion that their home isn't perfect. But what are you to do if they are positively insulted by even a request to have it staged?

The answer, of course, is to tread lightly. Don't insist, suggest. Sometimes it's helpful to bring in another, more-experienced agent to walk through the home and make suggestions about what needs to be done. You may also want to suggest that the sellers read a book on selling that describes the advantages of fixing up a property and getting it ready. (Of course, I think my *Tips & Traps When Selling a Home* would be a good choice!)

Usually any argument that sellers may have against staging falls apart when you point out that they need to see their home, not through their eyes, but through a buyer's eyes. What works personally for them may not work for someone else. When they bought the home, they immediately individualized it, made it specific for their needs and wants. Now they have to make it more public. They have to de-individualize it. (See below on suggestions about what to do to stage a property.)

What Should Be Done as Part of the Staging?

Although you may have lots of ideas on the subject of staging, you, as a new agent getting started, may not clearly know what works and what doesn't. As mentioned previously, bringing in a more-experienced agent will help.

Nevertheless, it may fall to you to come up with suggestions on what should be done to stage a home. When that happens here are some standards to fall back upon.

TIP

Curb appeal refers to that first impression that a house makes on a buyer. If it's positive, you'll have a much easier time selling the property. If it's negative, you'll spend most of your time trying to overcome it. Remember, you don't get a second chance to make a good first impression.

Standard Staging Techniques: Curb Appeal

- Trim back hedges, bushes, and flowers so that the front of the home is more visible.
- Green the lawn with watering and fertilizer; be sure it's well mowed and trimmed.
- Repaint the front of the house, along with the trim and especially the front door.
- Be sure that all front windows are clean.
- Clean off the driveway.
- Be sure there are no cars, trucks, wagons, tools, or anything else on the front lawn or driveway.
- Do what ever else is necessary to make the house look neat, tidy, and inviting to a buyer.

Standard Staging Techniques: Interior

- Remove at least a third of the furniture. Have it stored off the property. (Don't store it in closets or the garage, as it will make those areas look small.) This effort will make the home look bigger and more appealing.

- Paint any walls that have marks on them. (Cleaning often just makes the mess worse.)

- Have the carpets thoroughly cleaned or, if possible, replaced.

- Make sure the entry is spotless; clean floor tiles, and replace any that are broken.

- Remove most personal pictures from the home. Potential buyers want to imagine *their* family in the house, not be reminded of the seller's!

- Ask the sellers to remove all pots, pans, dishes, and so on from the kitchen countertops during showings. Be sure the countertop is spotless. Clean the kitchen cabinet doors if necessary.

- Clean the sink, and ask the sellers to make sure it's empty during showings.

- Clean the appliances, and ask the sellers to be sure to wash dishes frequently so the dishwasher remains empty during showings. Get rid of any stains and drip marks on the stove and in the oven.

- Replace bulbs throughout the house with the maximum wattage the fixtures will allow. Bring in extra light fixtures to remove shadows from any dark areas. Ask the sellers to be sure to turn on all lights before showings.

- Have all bathrooms thoroughly cleaned, especially removing any stains from toilets, sinks, tubs, and showers.

- Be sure any black mold is removed. Caution sellers about problems with black mold and about proper removal.

TRAP

Black mold is the latest, greatest fear among most home buyers. So many horror stories have been told about housing having to be destroyed because of infestation and of mitigation workers in bubble suits removing the black mold. Many buyers will simply avoid any home having even a hint of it. While, as of this writing, the Center for Disease Control has not spoken definitively about the mortal dangers of black mold, if any, it certainly can be a problem for those with allergies. It would be wise to educate sellers as to the near hysteria surrounding the problem. Request that, if they see any black mold, which is usually found in wet areas such as bathrooms and kitchen, they have it checked out and properly removed. (Often a termite and fungus infestation company can issue a report on it and handle removal.) Also note that the sellers should disclose the existence of any black mold, its removal, and how it was removed to buyers to help avoid problems down the road.

- Try to get the sellers to remove half of what's in their closets, if possible. Cluttered closets make buyers think the home doesn't have enough storage space.

- Ask sellers to keep the temperature around 70 degrees when the house is showing by using the heat or the air conditioning. Studies have shown that a slightly cool temperature encourages buyers to purchase.

- Clean windows, window sills, and window coverings.

- Do whatever else it takes to get the house into tip-top shape.

How Do You Find People to Stage Property?

In some communities, professional stagers are available. They usually will contact you through your office. Ask your broker/manager or other agents if they know of anyone who does it and if they can make a recommendation. (Not all stagers do terrific work!)

If all that you want is a basic "clean and run," you can find maid services in the phone book. Typically, they will charge something like $100 for two to four hours. They usually show up with a crew of three or four. For a couple of hundred dollars you can have the entire house cleaned and washed in just a day. This may be all that's required—and all that your budget allows!

For more elaborate work, such as painting, carpet cleaning, and window washing, you may need to hire individuals, if a stager, who would normally handle this, is not available. Virtually every agent who has been in the business for five years or more knows companies who do this type of work. Ask them who they recommend to sellers or who they perhaps themselves use on a regular basis. Ask some of the more-experienced agents.

Finally, if you can't find the right people to do the work, look up a property management company and call them. They have this work done all the time, and they will probably be happy to give you a recommendation.

When Should It Be Done?

Ideally the house should be staged before it's shown to the first buyer. Remember the warning concerning curb appeal and first impressions? I've shown houses that were in poor shape to buyers who turned them down, when I've known full well that if the houses were in great shape, they would have been accepted. You will be doing a disservice to your seller and to yourself if you allow a house in bad shape to be shown to anyone other than an investor.

TIP

Investors usually don't care what shape the home is in. They are looking for a property they can make money on either by flipping, or by holding and renting out. Indeed, they usually prefer to see properties that haven't yet been staged, hoping to get in early with a lowball offer that the seller might accept.

By all means try to get the home in shape before you hold a "broker's open" or before setting the house up as a caravan stop. While most brokers can quickly see beyond the surface dirt and mess to the home beneath, they may not be willing to show the house until it's been fixed up and cleaned. That's an unnecessary delay and results in the need for you to make contact with them a second time. Get it right the first time.

How Much Is Just Enough?

Finally, there's the matter of how much staging is just enough for a home. Perhaps you've gone through houses where the entryway was attractive, the kitchen was spotless, the bathrooms were clean, the rooms were tidy and not cluttered, only to come to the laundry area where clothes were scattered all over, the machines were rattling away, and the floor was dirty. That one area undid all the goodwill built up by the rest of the house.

The answer to how much is just enough, is that it's never enough. Get the entire house staged. Do as much as your budget and the seller's patience will allow.

Think of the example of selling steaks. Most people feel that a good steak is one of the best treats for the palette—even in an age of watching fat calories. But how do you sell a steak, short of cutting off a piece and offering it to a potential buyer?

The answer, of course, is that you don't sell the steak. You sell the sizzle. You show that steak sizzling away on a barbecue and immediately the odor, the taste, the smell come to the minds of those who see it. In other words, in order to sell steak you must show it at its mouth-watering best.

The same holds true for a house. You may have a top-quality house, but if you try to sell it in its raw condition, you'll get negative reactions, and offers may be for only a fraction of the price that the house could bring if it were fixed up.

No, it's not your house. But, it is your commission. The sooner the house sells, and the more money it sells for, the sooner you'll get that commission check . . . and the bigger that check will be.

14

Agent's Taxes and Insurance

Most agents who are getting started find their tax status something of a puzzlement. If they've been working for an employer for most of their previous career, now, suddenly they find they are working for themselves. This status appears to be a contradiction in terms, since they are, presumably, at the same time working for a broker in a realty company.

TIP

The tax rules are constantly changing. This chapter is designed to give you a general overview of what your requirements may be at the time of writing. But you should not rely solely on this material. You should consult with an accountant or tax attorney.

The confusion arises because of how the Internal Revenue System (IRS) categorizes most agents. They are called *independent contractors* for tax purposes.

An independent contractor is essentially someone who works for himself or herself. They determine what their daily routine will be, they decide how they will go about generating business, and they mainly set their own goals. Does this sound like the job description of a real estate salesperson?

The broker, of course, provides the environment within which the agent can operate—typically an office with phones, computers, advertising, and so on. Yet, unlike a true employer, the broker does not tell the agent exactly how to conduct business, how to process leads, or how to make money.

If this still sounds confusing, think of an author who writes a book for a publisher. The publisher determines the deadline when the book is due, how long it should be, the title, and even the cover blurbs. But it's up to the author to fill that book with any words he or she chooses. The author is an independent contractor with roughly the same relationship to the publisher as an agent (salesperson) has to a broker.

A similar example would be that of a consultant. The person who hires the consultant often will specify the parameters of the work to be done, the time frame, and even the amount of payment. Yet, it's entirely up to the consultant to come up with how to do the work.

Pay Ramifications of Being an Employee

Probably close to 95 percent of real estate agents are independent contractors. The remaining few are actual employees who work directly under an employer. It's important to understand the differences in terms of getting paid.

The employee will get a paycheck, typically every two weeks. This check comes whether or not the employee has made any deals. (Although, if over a period of time the employee doesn't make any deals, it's unlikely the employer will keep him or her on the job.)

From that paycheck the employer is required to deduct several things, including:

- *Withholding.* The employee fills out a W-4 form, and the employer withholds a certain amount of money from each paycheck to go toward the federal and state governments as income tax.

- *Federal Insurance Contributions Act (FICA).* In addition, the employer also withholds a certain amount of money to go toward social security taxes each pay period.

- *Medicare.* The employer also withholds money to go toward the employee's federal medicare account.

- *Other deductions.* Finally, the employer may withhold money, under the employee's direction, to go toward retirement accounts (401K, IRA, and so on). And there may be other federal, state, or local withholding as required.

If you've essentially always worked for an employer, all of this is quite familiar to you. You're well aware that no matter how big the amount you make, it's what you clear after all deductions—your take-home pay—that counts. And sometimes that amount can seem woefully small.

Pay Ramifications of Being an Independent Contractor

For the majority of people, becoming a real estate agent changes all that. Even though you work for a real estate broker, indeed may be *required* to serve a several-year apprenticeship, you are considered an independent contractor for tax purposes.

What that means is that when you get a commission check the only things that are typically taken out are your split with your broker and perhaps a franchise fee. Other than that, you get the whole commission to which you are entitled. There are usually *no deductions.*

As a result, the check is often quite substantial, certainly much higher than if you were an employee getting a paycheck from which deductions for taxes, social security, and other things had been taken.

TRAP

Don't immediately spend all your commission checks! Remember, you still have to pay taxes on that money.

The vital point to remember is that just because your broker didn't take out for taxes and so on, doesn't mean that you don't owe that money. You still do. Only, it's now up to you to pay it yourself.

How to Pay Your Own Taxes

Federal and state governments require you to pay taxes on your income on a quarterly basis, that's roughly every three months, except for the last installment, which is due a month later and the second installment which is due a month earlier. The payments are due January 15, April 15, June 15, and September 15.

You'll be required to estimate how much you'll owe in taxes for the year and then pay one quarter of it in each installment. Your taxes will include federal income tax, FICA, and Medicare to the federal government and state income taxes to your state.

TRAP

 I strongly urge you to obtain the services of a good accountant, at least when you're first starting out. It can be extremely difficult to guesstimate your tax liability when you're getting commissions on an irregular basis. And failure to make timely payments can result in interest and penalties.

In order to calculate your tax liability, you'll need to know not only your income, which now presumably is mainly composed of commissions, but also your real estate–related expenses. It's important to remember that as an agent, you're allowed to deduct a great number of expenses that an ordinary employee cannot. These *may* include the following, depending on your tax situation (see your accountant)[*]:

- *Auto expense.* There are specific guidelines for deductibility, whether you purchase outright or lease. In recent years, there have also been very generous write-offs on new-car purchases; see your accountant.

TIP

 If you take a deduction for business mileage, you must account for every mile. This is especially important when the car is used in part for business and in part for pleasure. A log of car use is usually a good solution.

- *Business cards, signs, lock boxes.* These can be deductible when they are used in the normal course of business.
- *Advertising.* This is usually deductible when you pay for it for the benefit of your business activity.

---

[*]Note: You must actually pay for these. You cannot take a deduction for something your broker or someone else pays for.

- *Home staging.* If, in fact, you actually pay for this work and are not reimbursed by the seller or your broker, you can probably deduct it.

- *Real estate investment.* There are specific advantages that an agent enjoys; see your accountant.

- *Any other legitimate expenses.* These expenses may encompass an enormous range, some of which are in gray areas;

TRAP

In most cases you cannot take a deduction for your clothing, even though agents normally must wear "dress" clothes to conduct business. One exception is usually when your broker requires you to wear, for example, a jacket with the name of the agency emblazoned on it.

You won't know your true income from real estate until you've calculated and deducted all of your legitimate expenses. Then, of course, your true income is subject to personal deductions, deductions for Simplified Employee Pension–Individual Retirement Accounts (SEP-IRAs; see below), and other accounts. While the calculation of taxes is not as complex as it may seem at first glance, it is tricky. That's why I repeatedly suggest that when getting started you use the services of a good accountant or tax attorney. And use these services early in the game, not just before your taxes are due.

TRAP

One of the biggest tax mistakes that new agents make is to make insufficient quarterly tax payments. Then, "suddenly" on April 15, they discover they owe a huge amount of money plus interest and penalties. As soon as you get that first commission, set aside the amount you need for taxes.

What About Retirement?

As an independent contractor, it is generally up to you to set up your own retirement, although, in some cases, a broker may offer a retirement plan. This, however, is usually not too difficult as SEP-IRA plans are available, which allow you to set aside a substantial portion of your income on a pretax basis, up to certain maximum amounts.

Although it's usually difficult, with all your other expenses, to even think about setting aside money for retirement when you're starting out, I suggest you at least set up the account, even if all you can set aside for the year is a hundred dollars. Getting into the habit will make it much easier to put more aside when later on your commission checks grow.

What About Health Insurance?

While you can attempt to buy health insurance for you and your family on an individual basis, you'll probably find that it's very expensive and, in some cases, difficult to get, if not impossible. For that reason, many brokers offer an office plan. This is particularly the case with franchises.

Here, typically after working with the company for a few months, you may be able to buy into the plan. The coverage varies enormously, and there may be restrictions for pre-existing conditions. As most of us now realize, insurance companies seem to prefer to "cherry-pick." They want the young and the healthy and not the older and those with illnesses. Unfortunately, this latter group is the one that most needs health coverage.

Therefore, my suggestion is that even if you're young and healthy, you buy into a health plan. It will probably be inexpensive and then, later on when you get older and, perhaps, ill, you'll (it is hoped!) be covered.

What About Liability Insurance?

As a real estate agent, you'll be dealing with huge amounts of money, property, and personal feelings. Most times, things will go well and there will be no problems. But, occasionally, sometimes in spite of your best efforts, something goes awry. Then come the lawsuits.

TRAP

When a seller or buyer sue, typically they sue everyone involved in the deal, whether that person caused the problem or not. That means that as an agent, you must be prepared to pay for the costs of defending yourself, even if you eventually win the case. Today, defense costs can easily run into the tens of thousands of dollars.

Liability insurance for agents is called E&O, for "Errors and Omissions," and, basically, it covers what it says. In most cases, if you're sued, the insurance company will provide legal representation and defense. And if the other party wins, it will pay damages, up to the limitations of the policy.

You need E&O insurance. There should be no debate about this. However, it should be provided by your broker. (Brokers need it even more than you do!)

However, since E&O can be expensive, depending on the loss history of your broker, you may be asked to pay a share of it out of your commissions. This payment is something that you can negotiate with your broker, and you should determine when you first sign on (see Chapter 3).

Some agents think that their homeowner's insurance will cover them for liability in their business. In some cases, this may actually be true, as when you operate a business out of your home. But a lot will be determined by your insurance policy (what it says it will cover) and the reason for the complaint. For example, someone tripping on a step while getting into your home office might be covered. Someone suing you over negligence when writing up a purchase offer might not.

Remember all that freedom we talked about in the early chapters that you achieve when you get to be an agent? Well, that also includes freedom to not have an employer hold your hand on taxes and insurance matters. Here, you're really on your own. And you would do well to make sure your taxes are properly paid and your insurance needs are appropriately covered.

15

Emerging Business Models

Dramatic change is sweeping through the real estate industry. Traditional businesses are being challenged by an onslaught of newer, more nimble models. While buying and selling property won't ever disappear, the rules governing real estate agency transactions are being rewritten as we speak.

For years, it was common for buyer and seller agents to split a 6 percent commission. However, there is nothing standard anymore. Today, agents may only get 5 percent, 4 percent, not get paid a commission at all but instead work for salary, or not even enter into the equation.

That isn't to say that we are on the verge of real estate agent extinction. Quite contrary, these new business models represent new opportunities for the savvy real estate agent. By staying in step with the market, the successful real estate agent will have more potential than ever to capitalize from emerging business models.

The Incredible Shrinking Commission

While as agents know there is no "standard" commission rate in the industry, most agents charge between 5 and 6 percent. (In the Northwest that rate is sometimes lower.) At 5 percent, this means on a $300,000 house the total commission is $15,000 (typically 2.5 percent for the buyer's agent and 2.5 percent for the seller's agent).

Things, however, are changing. The advent of the Internet is threatening the traditional way of doing business in real estate. These days, it is much easier for a house hunter to search online listings for available properties. This makes the old, thick MLS books that were historically a big value-added of agents, a thing of the past.

Even beyond listings, the Internet enables easy access to important investment considerations like comparable sales, school rankings, crime statistics, proximity to shopping and freeways, and all sorts of other important information. Previously, buyers would be heavily dependent on an agent for this information.

OK, so it is clear that the Internet is making information much easier to get. But how does this translate to lower commission rates?

To answer this question, let's consider several typical activities performed by the real estate agent:

As this diagram illustrates, the activities can be broadly categorized according to level of technical know-how and time to complete. The activities that fall in the lower left-hand quadrant—easy, along both axes—will be the first to be "stolen" from the real estate agent. We have already seen many different Internet sites pop up that provide

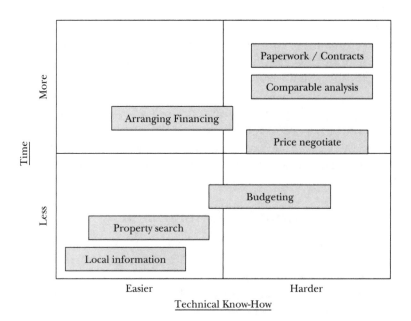

Figure 15.1 Subset of Agent Activities

both local information and property searches. In contrast, the activities in the upper right-hand corner—harder, along both axes—will likely remain dominated by the real estate agent. These are usually more complex tasks that require the skill and expertise of a trained professional. Clients will probably not want to take risks with these activities, as any error can potentially cost lots of money.

As the role of the agent decreases, the amount he or she can charge as a commission correspondingly decreases. Combine the Internet with intensified competition from an increasing number of agents that work in the market and it is easy to see why commissions are shrinking.

Discount Brokers

Brokerage houses that compete on commission are commonly referred to as discount brokers. These agents will lower their commissions to woo away clients from competitors. The obvious cost of this practice is that discount brokers will make less money per transaction than their counterparts. Therefore, they must close more deals in order to make the same amount of money. This is why discounting may work only if you feel somewhat confident in your ability to handle a very large amount of business. (Remember also that competitors may retaliate with even lower prices. In this way, you can enter into a price war from which everyone may be worse off than they were at the beginning.)

Another type of discount broker is the Internet-based company that enables "shopping" among different real estate agents. This type

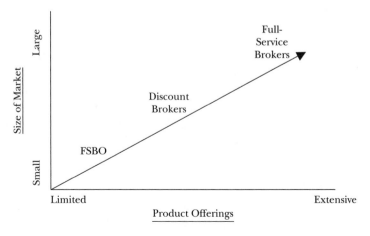

Figure 15.2 Spectrum of Business Models

of player enables potential buyers and sellers to surf for the lowest commission rates. So, someone with a house for sale in a hot market can get quotes quickly from half a dozen offices in the area.

Discounted Fees

Another interesting wrinkle in the commission game is the discounted fee. This is the idea that an agent or office returns a reward to a client after closing. Discounted fees are promoted through giant retailers along the model first pioneered with regard to the sale of new automobiles. (See a contracted dealer for a lower price or, in this case, a lower commission or, in some cases, a cash bonus to the buyer.) The promise for the agent or office is a plethora of leads. The cost is a discounted commission and perhaps some form of referral fee to the retailer.

The discounted fee can come in a variety of forms. One that seems obvious is a lower commission to a seller. But a truly savvy real estate office may partner with other local businesses to form an alliance. For example, if you arrange a deal with a local paint store, you can offer your clients coupons to the paint store. The paint store will give them discounts on their paint orders within a few months of the purchase of their new homes.

TIP

 The average purchaser of a resale home spends more than $10,000 on painting and remodeling during the first six months of ownership.

Lets look at an illustration of how the pain—in terms of financial cost—can be defused in order to provide greater benefits to both the clients and agents in a deal. Let's see what happens to the same $300,000 house sale, assuming a 5 percent commission, under three different scenarios: no discounted commission, discount to seller, and a coupon (as with the paint store in the example above).

Fee for Service

Rather than being the single source for the complete transaction, some offices will slice and dice the real estate agents' functions into individually packaged and sold units. In this manner, people can hire

	Clients	Agents	Third Party
No Discount	– $15,000	+ $15,000	
Advantages: Most people are familiar and comfortable with this scenario. It is the easiest to manage because it does not require returning cash after the close or partnering with other businesses			
$5,000 Discounted Commission	– $10,000	+ $10,000	
Advantages: It may be easy to attract new clients by offering a discount if you are able to close on their real estate deal. If you are able to increase the number of transactions, you may be able to ultimately net greater profits under this scenario.			
$5,000 Partner Coupon	– $10,000	+ $12,500	– $2,500
Advantages: The client benefits from a major discount while the cost is distributed between the agent and the partnering business. Agents win from possibly attracting more business and third party businesses benefit from new customers.			

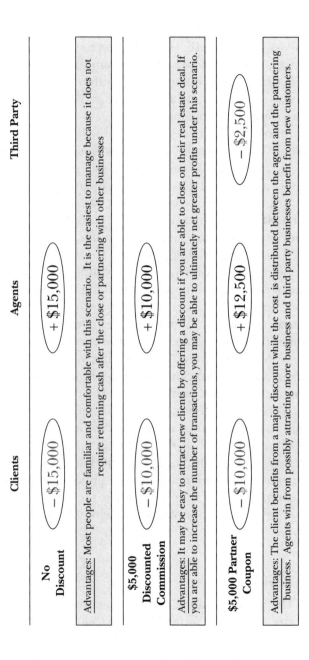

Figure 15.3 Impact of Coupons on Client and Agent Costs

experts to write up the paperwork after selling a home for sale by owner (FSBO) as the only agent contribution.

Many of the work-for-hire offices are starting to charge clients by the hour rather than work on a percentage commission. Although this may seem like a scary proposition to the budding real estate agent, consider that you may, in fact, be able to earn more on an hourly basis through a work-for-hire arrangement.

The key to unlocking the benefits of an hourly pay scenario lies in an idea known as "moral hazard." Simply defined, this concept refers to the risk that, after a set commission payment has been agreed upon, the client can demand a lot of attention and resources with no additional reward to the agent. For example, say you agree to sell two different $300,000 homes for two different people. The first rarely calls your office and leaves the details of the sale in your hands. The other person is constantly calling you and is a huge drain on your time. Even though the second person is costing you more (in the form of time, energy, and so on) you are making the same amount of money on both deals.

In an hourly arrangement, there is no incentive for a client to place ridiculous demands on your time. In fact, the contrary is true, as each hour they make you work, they are increasing your fees. Under this arrangement, the smart agent can actually net more money than if he or she were on a commission basis.

An additional benefit to the pay-per-hour model is that the agent gets paid regardless of the outcome of the sale price. In other words, the agent does not need to close the deal to get paid. This is great for both the agent and the client. For the agent, hourly fees reduce the overall risk in your job and make the revenue stream more predictable. For clients, there is no incentive for the real estate agent to rush the deal or settle on a poor offer just to close. Both parties can, in fact, benefit here.

TRAP

The great downside to a fee for service or an hourly service is liability. Your ultimate liability in case something goes awry in a deal may be the same whether you get $200 for a short consultation or $15,000 for a full commission. Of course, E&O insurance can somewhat mitigate this concern.

Salaried Salespeople

Another new model that threatens the traditional commission-based real estate world is that of salaried salespeople. The analogy here can be easily seen in relation to your local electronics store. Many electronics stores have tended away from a commission-based compensation program as a way to actually increase the customer service provided by their salespeople. The idea is that reducing the pressure to "sell" actually makes the salesperson more effective and provides an overall better shopping experience to the customer. In other words, changing the compensation model turns the people on the floor into paid consulting experts rather than pressuring salespeople. Several national discount brokerage firms are now offering this model.

In the real estate world, salaries can be very useful to an agent. One of the main advantages is revenue smoothing. In other words, agents working on commission have no way of forecasting or planning their revenue. In some months they may make lots of money after closing several deals, but other months may be completely dry. With a salary, you can know exactly how much money to expect regardless of your transactions.

TIP

If you've previously always worked as an employee, the salaried salesperson model may strongly appeal to you. You'll instinctively recognize and understand it.

On the flip side, salaries can make for a pay ceiling and limit the amount a salesperson could potentially earn. Why should you work hard and try to sell a lot of houses if you are going to get paid the same amount as if you sold just a few?

For this reason, the most enticing emerging pay scale involves both a salary and a commission. The salary is a great benefit because it is the floor (the least amount of money you will make), while the commission is the boundless pay based on performance. If you sell nothing, you get the base salary, but if you sell dozens of homes, you could make a lot. Amounts earned with the combination of salary and commission tends to be less than amounts for an agent working strictly on commission. (Note: We're not speaking here of a "draw" against commission that some brokers will work out for salespeople.)

Comparing the Different Models

Each type of compensation model must provide its own benefits, or else it wouldn't exist. Let's take a closer look at what the real estate agent can hope to gain by working in a pure commission, hybrid model, and pure salary environment:

Financial benefit is only one component (albeit an important one!) of the real estate agent's compensation consideration. Another has to do with risk. An agent who is completely dependent on commissions to pay the bills is putting a huge amount of pressure on himself or herself to deliver. What if the market turns bad, the agent gets

Table 15.1 Comparing Different Business Models

Pure Commission	Hybrid	Pure Salary
The agent makes no money if he or she does not close any deals. But the agent's pay increases proportionally to the number of transactions managed.	The agent receives a base salary plus a performance-based bonus commission. The graph for this model looks a little different than for pure commission. Now, instead of intersecting at zero (that is, no deals equals no pay), the line intersects the x axis at the base salary pay. In other words, the agent makes money regardless of what deals are made, because of the salary. Despite the base salary, however, there is no limit to what he or she can make as the number of deals increases.	The graph for pure salary model looks quite different from the others. In this scenario, the agent makes the exact same amount of money regardless of the number of deals he or she manages. The amount of pay is set and does not vary.
The slope of the line will depend on the agent's commission percentage. For example, a high commission of 7 percent will look much steeper than a 5 percent commission rate, as the former will result in more cash more quickly than the latter.		
(The pay scale does not need to be a linear line. The amount an agent earns may actually increase or decrease as he or she makes more sales.)		

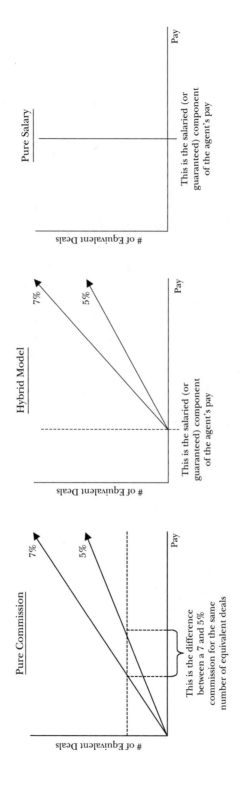

sick, or bad luck lends itself to a less-than-stellar year? In these cases, the agent may be left high and dry. For this reason, it is important to consider the risk of each of the above models to the agent.

By plotting each of the three models (pure commission, hybrid model, and pure salary), we can see the relative difference in risk to the agent. Therefore, we can plainly see that pure commission offers the most risk while pure salary is the safest.

Why Aren't There More of These Emerging Businesses?

You may be asking, "If these new business models can offer greater opportunities to new agents, why aren't there more of them?" That is a great question, and the answer may not be as obvious as it seems.

First, the entrenched mega-brokerage players in the industry undoubtedly do not want to see a drop in revenue from lower commission rates. As a result, they may insist that their agents uphold the higher rates. And it has been implied, although this suggestion can be very difficult to substantiate, that, just to discourage adoption of this new business model, predatory action may be taken against brokerage firms that offer discounts.

TIP

It is always difficult for a newcomer to challenge the business model of the incumbent.

Second, despite the National Association of Realtors (NAR) publishing that the number of people using an agent has actually increased from 77 percent to 83 percent over the years 1999 to 2003, more people may in fact be choosing alternative brokering methods, which are not separated out in the NAR study.

Third, changing the infrastructure in such a huge market is a slow and daunting task. With a price tag for homes in the hundreds of thousands of dollars, most people do not want to take risks when it comes to buying and selling them and, hence, opt for the tried-and-true traditional agent experience.

In the future, agents should expect clients to negotiate more frequently on commission rates. It may be some time before we see commission prices fall systematically across all industry players, but the wheels seem to be in motion. Just as we saw transaction costs plummet in equity trading, we can expect the same in the future of the real estate market. And while that change scares a great many in the industry, it also may make millionaires out of those willing to embrace the emerging business models.

16

Become Your Own Broker?

The Holy Grail for nearly everyone who goes into real estate is to become their own broker and open their own office. As those in the field know, the vast majority of newcomers start out as salespeople and are required to serve an apprenticeship, typically several years. Only after that period of time can they apply for and receive—after taking a test—a broker's license and work independently. (Those with college degrees, in some states, can step right up into the broker's position.)

The big advantage to working independently is that you don't have to work under the tutelage of a broker. You can be your own boss and run your own business the way you see fit. Further, you no longer have to split those commissions with a broker. *Everything* that you make belongs to you! You can become your own man or woman.

Sounds great, doesn't it?

But it's not necessarily all that it's cracked up to be. In this chapter we're going to look at what's involved in running your own real estate office—being your own broker.

TRAP

My own feeling is that most agents should *not* endeavor to become their own broker—or at least, not right away. It's far better to serve an apprenticeship of at least two and possibly as many as five years under a good broker in an active office. The experiences you get will be invaluable in helping you develop a long-term and profitable career.

TIP

Some people thrive on independence. It's the *only* way they can function to the fullest. If you're one of those, then you should consider becoming your own broker and having your own office.

Is There an Advantage to Being a Broker?

Naturally, when you work with your clients, it's much more gratifying to say that you're the broker, not the salesperson. You can have your cards printed with the word *broker* or *Realtor* as opposed to *salesperson* or *agent* or *Associate*. If nothing else, *you'll* know what you are, and that may help you to speak with more authority.

The problem is that 90 percent of the people with whom you deal are unlikely to know the difference. Either you're their real estate agent or you're not. So, there's often no advantage to being a broker from the point of making an impression on those clients.

For that other 10 percent, however, the distinction can be important. They are usually the more sophisticated clients, often investors. They will want to know that you're a broker, even if you've got your license parked under another broker (discussed shortly). They want to be dealing with the "top dog," not someone lower down on the food chain.

And, as noted, when you're your own broker and have your own office, you can set policy, collect commissions, and generally run the roost. I've been my own broker for a great many years, and can testify that it can give you a good feeling.

Advantages of Being Your Own Broker

- You can set up and run your own office, either as an independent or as a franchisee.
- You can tell your clients, who might be impressed.
- You can collect commissions and not necessarily have to split them with another broker.
- You can be your own person, to a large extent.

Is There a Disadvantage to Being a Broker?

The downside of being your own broker, however, is rarely seen or understood by salespeople. But it definitely exists. It's often financial, and it can involve coming up with the capital to get started; it includes not only what's required to set up an office but also your own living expenses until your cash flow begins. It can also involve having to meet monthly expenses. And, if you build your office and have salespeople, it can involve coaching and taking time out from your own schedule to help them.

TRAP

One of the biggest hidden problems of being your own broker is isolation. You may not have anyone with whom you can consult either about problem deals or about your own finances and other concerns.

Here are some of the difficulties with working for yourself as a broker.

- If you operate as an independent, you seldom have someone else to go to for help when you get into unfamiliar territory. (State and national real estate associations can provide some assistance.)

- If you operate as a franchisee, you often must submit to the policies of the franchiser.

- You usually have a monthly "nut" to crack—a financial overhead for office expenses, advertising, legal fees, insurance, and so on.

- You may need a substantial capital investment to get started.

- If you work as a franchisee, you may have a minimum deal or dollar target you must hit.

What's Involved in Being a Broker?

I have two friends who became brokers within the last few years. Their stories are markedly different but very instructive.

Both Alice and Paul got their salesperson licenses and went to work for the same broker, a franchise operation. They received extensive training and aid from more experienced agents. (It was a terrific office, one of the top ones in the county.)

Both started off slowly, but by the end of their first year both were making substantial commissions and selling many properties. By the end of their second year, both Alice and Paul were earning well into six figures, driving luxury cars, and were considered top producers. Then, both decided to get their broker's licenses.

Alice opened up her own independent office in a big way. She worked hard to make it grow. Paul decided to start out slowly and see how things went. Their stories are indicative of what can be involved in setting up shop as your own broker.

Alice's Story

Alice quickly decided that success for her meant building a large office. She had made it a point of meeting many of the newer agents both from her old office and from other offices in the area. Now, she solicited them and asked them to join with her. She said she was building the biggest independent office in the city and offered them an opportunity to get in on the ground floor. And she offered them a slightly better split than they were getting from their old offices. Many of them took her up on her offer.

She needed a physical location, of course, and she chose a corner suite in a prominent local outdoor mall. It was bigger than a strip mall, but not a full shopping center, and it offered both a popular grocery store chain and movie theater as anchors. Her office signs faced in two directions, so that people could see both entering and exiting the mall.

She had nearly 10,000 square feet of office space that she leased at a hefty fee for three years. And she outfitted this space with top-of-the-line furniture. She also had three conference rooms with luxurious tables and chairs. And she provided the latest computers for all of her people, not to mention a state-of-the-art phone system. She required all of her agents to carry cell phones, but she gave them a small allowance to help defray the costs. And she hired a receptionist to field questions and direct clients who came in the front door.

Then she began an aggressive advertising campaign that featured listed properties in the local biweekly newspaper. She took out a full-page ad in each issue.

Needless to say, this all cost money. Behind the scenes, Alice mortgaged her own home and sold two rentals that she had acquired in previous years. She also borrowed money from a rich relative and took out a personal loan at the bank. She managed to raise a million and a half dollars. This, however, was only enough to get her started and keep her going for a few months!

Alice was under the gun. She had to get deals, lots of them, and fast. So she made strong demands on her salespeople. They all were given sales targets. Since she picked the top producers of the new crop of agents, deals did quickly start rolling in.

But not all the agents were able to keep up. And those that weren't, she quickly replaced with others. Within six months she had a stable of nearly a dozen top producers, and she had boosted her office into the position of number-two producer in her area.

TRAP

There was a huge amount of activity in Alice's office. However, her churn-and-burn attitude with salespeople made it a cutthroat place to work. As a result, her salespeople turnover was high.

Alice's overhead was enormous, and although the deals and commissions came pouring in, it was still a fight to keep things going. She imposed a $500 "administrative fee" on each deal. Her salespeople protested that they had difficulty getting sellers and buyers to pop for this, but she insisted. After all, she had a huge financial nut to crack. So more money came in.

Alice kept things going for a full year, when she stepped back to analyze where she was. She now had 13 full-time agents working for her and was sometimes processing dozens of deals a month. She had hired a mortgage broker and an escrow clerk. She had a staging crew and other support staff. To anyone looking in, she was an extremely successful real estate broker.

But there was a personal toll to all this. She was working 70 to 80 hours a week. She was making almost no deals on her own—all her time was spent running her office, coaching her salespeople, helping with closings, and putting out fires that kept cropping up with difficult deals. Further, one of her agents had mishandled a client and the state real estate commissioner had stepped in because of a complaint. The salesperson's license was suspended and Alice, as the broker who was supposed to maintain supervision, was given a warning. There was the threat of a lawsuit and Alice's E&O insurance made a payout to settle. As a result, her insurance premiums tripled.

What was worse, what with paying down her debts and keeping up with her expenses, she wasn't taking home a lot more money than she had made when she was working full-time as a salesperson for another broker. She was surprised to find that she was running herself ragged, yet not really accomplishing as much as she had thought.

Alice, however, was a smart and resourceful person. So she picked one of her best agents, also a broker, and made that person office manager. Now someone else had the responsibilities, supervision, and headaches of day-to-day operations. Alice just handled the most difficult and problematic deals. She also began getting back into the business with her own listings and sales.

Alice kept her office growing and opened two more in the next five years, until she was number one in the area. Then she sold out to—not paid into—a franchise company for enough money to retire comfortably, if she chose to. Instead, however, she continued to work in her original office as a broker, hanging the license under the franchise company, still taking care of the most difficult deals, as well as working on her own.

Alice was a success story; she had made her fortune by growing a real estate business. However, she had realized when to let others take over. She had successfully made the transitions from entrepreneur to manager to founder.

Paul's Story

Paul took a different tack. He opened a small independent office. He quickly staffed it with three salespeople whom he had met working for his last broker. These three weren't all top producers, but they provided a steady flow of deals. More important to Paul, he respected them and their work.

Paul opened his office in a much smaller strip mall than Alice's office. It was at the back of the mall, so his rent was low. He bought secondhand office furniture and secondhand computers. He hired a part-time receptionist for weekends and used the phone company's cheapest system. All of his agents had cell phones, which they paid for entirely on their own. Paul also advertised in the local newspaper, but he bought short three- and four-line ads in the classified section.

Paul's office also grew, but it did so far more slowly than Alice's. At the end of three years he had five salespeople. He was also the office's top producer, pulling in the most listings and making the most deals.

The problem he had was that there were several franchise companies located nearby. Their advertising far exceeded anything he could
match. They had many more agents, typically the more aggressive
ones. And they seemed to have lots of capital to keep them going.

Things came to a head when Paul's office ran into a dry spell. Real
estate in general had slowed down. And for no specific reason he could
identify, no one in the office seemed able to sell any property. Yes, they
had lots of listings, but no sales.

Two of the salespeople left, another took a part-time job, and the
remaining two who were older considered retiring. Paul had virtually no income for months on end and mortgaged his home in order
to meet his expenses.

Finally, he decided he had had enough. He closed his office and
went to work for one of the local franchise companies. He parked his
broker's license there and, not bothered with the managerial and
financial problems of running an office, began making deals. Soon he
was out of his financial hole and again earning a six-figure income.

Paul came to the conclusion that for him, being his own broker
and running his own office was not what he was cut out to do. He
did not have the will to put pressure on his salespeople to make
more deals, or to let them go. He did not have great entrepreneur-
ial skills. He was not a wonderful manager.

But he was a terrific real estate agent. The best lesson that Paul
learned was finding out what he did best. And sticking with it.

Should You Work for Another Broker?

Just because you get your real estate broker's license doesn't mean
you must open your own office. As you're probably aware, a great
many brokers work for other brokers. They work for independent
offices as well as franchisees.

Having a broker's license puts you in a better position to negotiate a better split with your office. The office manager/broker knows
that if you aren't happy, you can easily go somewhere else. It's not
quite so easy for a salesperson to switch offices.

Further, if you're a good producer and don't want to split with your
broker, you can make arrangements to simply pay for your desk space.
You'll be in the office and benefit from its image. You'll essentially pay
all of your own expenses. But, then when the commission check
comes in, all of it will be written to you. Many independents and at
least one national chain operate in this fashion.

TIP

There really is no downside to becoming a broker, as opposed to staying a salesperson. The cost is minimal, chiefly the fee for the test and license, and any study materials or courses that you need. It is one of the least expensive career advancement moves you can make.

Other Opportunities

Don't think that you are limited to being either a salesperson or a broker. It's important to examine all the possibilities in real estate. For example, you could become a mortgage broker. Many states have a separate exam to become one, although some, such as California, do not. You could earn fees for finding mortgages. Those who tend to know a lot of other agents who can refer people to them tend to do well in this area. As with any other job, however, it's wise to first serve an apprenticeship under an experienced mortgage broker. Besides, that is probably the best way to make contacts in the mortgage industry, which will be essential to your business.

You could also become an appraiser, a professional home inspector, an escrow officer, or any of dozens of other careers.

As noted in Chapter 1, there are ample opportunities in real estate. But often you won't realize what these are until you've spent some time selling. Get your feet wet in the business. Then, move on and up to where you fit the best—and where you want to go.

17

Everything You Really Need to Know to Succeed

Doing well in real estate does not involve learning something arcane. The techniques that will allow you to become a *super-agent* are not hidden or known only by a select few. In short, there are *no deep secrets.*

Most of what's involved is just common sense. The rest is refining your technique and keeping your nose to the grindstone. Just in case, if, after reading this far, you're still not sure what you should be doing, here are seven top tips for making it in a big way.

TIP

One *super-agent* I know put it this way: Becoming a successful real estate agent is 10 percent talent, 90 percent education, and 100 percent hard work.

Be Your Unique Self

We all have strengths—and weaknesses. If you always lead with your weaknesses, you'll probably improve them over time, but chances are you're not going to succeed very often. On the other hand, if you lead with your strengths, you'll not only get stronger, but chances are you will get to be more successful.

A perfect example is a good friend I have who is also an agent. Melinda knows both her strengths and her weaknesses. Her biggest strength is that she can almost instantly form rapport with a client. Indeed, after being with her for just half an hour, most people are ready to do business, either to give a listing or buy a home. It's positively amazing how she can get into the confidence of others to the point where they are dedicated to her. I've seen prospects who absolutely would not buy from anyone else except her, even after she's taken them out half a dozen times and they still haven't found quite the right property. The loyalty of her clients is legendary.

In short, she seems to be the perfect real estate agent. Except for her biggest weakness. Which is that she cannot fathom real estate forms. I have actually coached her on filling out a purchase agreement. Of course, she understands where to put in the buyers' names and the property's address. But, when there's a box to check, even something as simple as a finance contingency, she stumbles. "Do I check it if they're going to get financing from the seller? Or do I check it if they're getting it from a mortgage broker? How do I handle it if they're not pre-approved?"

We've gone over the forms dozens of times until she seems to have it perfectly clear. Then, when she's with a client, she becomes unsure and, often as not, fills it out incorrectly.

I don't know whether Melinda's problem stems from dyslexia, inability to concentrate, or some form of insecurity. Nevertheless, it's there.

The good part is that she realizes it. And she works around it.

When it comes time to sign a client to a listing or a purchase agreement or anything else, she brings them to her office and has either her broker or another experienced agent do the paperwork. While you might think this could raise issues with the client, cause them to lose confidence in Melinda, and make them less willing to sign, it doesn't. She uses her charm and her rapport and the clients melt in her hands, sometimes even *helping her* with the forms!

In short, Melinda recognizes where she's good … and where she's not so good. And she uses her strength to overcome her weakness.

You may not have trouble with forms. But maybe you have trouble establishing rapport. Regardless, chances are you're not strong in all areas. None of us is perfect. But, it's just as likely you are strong in one or a couple of areas.

Define yourself. Determine just where your strengths and weaknesses lie. And then always lead from strength.

TRAP

Be careful of following mentors too closely, whether they be a friendly more experienced agent, a seminarist, or even an author. Their strengths and weaknesses are not likely to be the same as yours. Hence, their advice, while useful, may not be completely applicable to you. Yes, you can learn from them. But, only you can learn about yourself.

Don't Be Afraid to Experiment Early

Many agents, when they first get started, operate under a kind of hidden panic. Yes, you need to get leads, convert them to listings, find prospects, convert them to buyers, make deals, and get your commissions. But you also are most likely to be under financial constraints. In the back of your mind you silently may be telling yourself, "I've only got five months to get this career off the ground—got to get going, quickly!" This leads to a panicky feeling.

Experiencing panic means that you stop thinking and instead start grasping at anything that seems to work. Another agent starts knocking on doors and the second day out gets a listing. "Aha," You say to yourself, "That's the way to go." And you start knocking on doors.

There's nothing wrong with doing this. The problem is that you could spend the next five months knocking on doors and still not get any listings.

It would be far better to make a list of all the possible ways that you could make deals. (Recheck the previous chapters for suggestions.) Then try them *all.*

Knocking on doors is one approach. Cold calling, though not preferred by this author, is another. You could approach friends and relatives, join organizations, contact old associates from previous jobs, try flyers, work the expired MLS listings, hit the FSBOs, and so on.

The point is, try everything. And try it more than once. You won't really know what works for you until you've given it a shot. And the sooner in your real estate career you do this, the better.

TRAP

Don't get stuck on only one or two approaches to selling property. If you do, you may run out of time and money before you become successful. Experience as much of the field as quickly as you can.

Select the Right Work Environment

In Chapter 3 we talked about finding just the right broker and office for you. It is hoped you'll follow the suggestions and will land in a perfect work environment.

But don't count on it. Sometimes, even though we think we've made the perfect choice, things just don't work out. We end up in a poor work environment.

How do you know whether or not you're in a poor work environment? Here are some characteristics of one:

- *Lack of emotional support from your broker.* He or she doesn't tell you what a good job you're doing, no "pats on the back," doesn't have time for you.

- *No help from your peers.* The experienced agents in the office don't have time or the inclination to go out of their way to help you get started.

- *Poor training program.* Presumably, after reading Chapter 3, you've picked an office with a training program. But, perhaps the trainer is weak, or the course is too short, or something else.

- *Lack of equipment.* You don't get an adequate desk, or a good computer and appropriate software, or a phone where the line isn't always busy, or signs and lockboxes, and so on.

- *Inadequate advertising.* You're counting on the broker's ads to help sell your listings and produce prospects. If there's little to no advertising, you're missing out an important avenue of making deals.

- *Negative criticism.* You're called a "poor producer," a "loser," a "wheel spinner," a "deep thinker," or similar terms, rather than given constructive help.

- *Other negatives.* The broker or office could have a bad reputation, or be in a poor location, or make unreasonable demands (set unrealistic target goals for you), and so on.

You have to decide whether your work environment is positive or negative. If it's the latter, then you should move elsewhere to a better environment. There are always other brokers and other offices. It's just that simple.

TRAP

Don't get caught trying to improve a bad work environment. This effort is something you can attempt as an experienced agent. But when just getting started, you need the work environment to help you out, not the other way round.

Work Hard at Every Task

I hate the term *wheel spinner,* even more than I do the word *loser.* The reason is that they both are forms of negative criticism; they're a way for someone of limited compassion and humanity to put another person down.

Nevertheless, at some point you are going to have to determine if you are actually working hard or just "spinning your wheels"—if you're really doing all that you can, or are mostly just spending time without being productive.

There are a lot of giveaways. Here are some wasted efforts that suggest you should be working harder:

- Frequent and extended trips to the coffee maker or water cooler.

- Being repetitive—doing the same task over and again instead of learning and improving.

- Spending too much time in the office, especially in gossiping with other agents.

- Spending too much time out of the office, especially on chores at home.

- Spending too much time touring properties, especially when you don't have a specific buyer in mind.

- Getting stuck on paperwork, especially filing, cleaning, and rearranging your desk.

TRAP

Remember, a cluttered desk often means a busy agent.

- Being ineffective—spending a lot of time at a task, such as farming, but not getting results.
- Cutting back on the hours you spend on real estate, especially cutting back on weekends.

Hard work should get results. If you're getting those big commission checks on a regular basis, then don't worry that you're not working hard enough. If, on the other hand, the checks aren't coming, then worry. And do something about it.

TIP

As Master Yoda (and hundreds of Zen masters before him) said in Star Wars, "Don't try—do."

Aim for the More Expensive Properties

We've discussed this topic before, but it's one of those things that bears repeating. Let's do the math again. Let's say that you're pulling in a 5 percent commission, which in some regions is a more realistic figure than 6 percent. And say, forgetting franchise fees for a moment, that you're splitting that amount in half with your broker.

You sell a $250,000 home, which is near the national average. Your take is going to be $6,250.

Commission at 5 Percent and 50-50 Split at $250,000

$250,000	Sales price
× .05	Commission rate (percentage)
12,500	Total commission
× .50	Broker split (percentage)
$ 6,250	Your cut

That's not a bad commission, and you should feel good about getting it. Now, let's say that instead of a quarter-million-dollar house, you sold a half-million-dollar house. Here's the commission split:

Commission at 5 Percent and 50-50 Split at $500,000

$500,000	Sales price
×____.05	Commission rate (percentage)
25,000	Total commission
×____.50	Broker split (percentage)
$ 12,500	Your cut

It's hard to argue against it being a whole lot nicer to get $12,500 than $6,250. What could you do with the extra six thousand dollars plus? I'm sure you could quickly develop a spending list. Furthermore, what if you sold a million-dollar property? Double the commission check again!

What's important to keep in mind here are three things that I've named after an agent friend of mine, Ted. Here are the three differences between selling a quarter-million-dollar house and a half-million-dollar house:

Time. All else being equal, there's no reason it should take an hour longer to list, find buyers for, write up the deal for, and close on the more expensive home.

Effort. If it doesn't take any more time, how could it possibly take any more effort?

Difficulty. Some say that a more expensive house is a more complex deal. Of course, that's possible, as when the more expensive property is a custom home with potential problems in clearing title or getting financing. But, that's the exception, rather than the rule. Today, there are $500,000 tract homes, particularly on the coasts. Indeed, there are multimillion-dollar tract homes in many parts of the country!

In short, introduce yourself to TED.

TIP

You'll make the kind of deals that you set your sights on. If you go for the cheaper properties, those are what you sell. Go for the more expensive properties, and you'll sell those. Remember, what we're really talking about here is not selling more, but selling smarter.

Get a Better Broker Split

This is something that every agent aims for from the day he or she starts out. It doesn't take much wit to know that you'll do a whole lot better if you get to claim 75 percent of the office commission rather than 50 percent. However, the trick is know *when* and *how* to get a bigger split.

There are two rules to follow here. The first is, don't ask for a bigger split until you can *demand* it. You can demand it when your productivity exceeds your broker's goals for you and surpasses the sales of your office "competitors."

You'll know when that is. One day you'll say to yourself, "Hey, if I'm doing so well, why am I still only getting a 50 percent split?" And then it's time to do something about it.

The second rule is, don't expect your broker to reward your good efforts by increasing your split on his or her own. It's the exceptional broker who will go out of his or her way to reward you by hiking your rate. (A few offices, of course, do have a policy where the commission split is determined by either the number of sales or the volume of income you produce.) After all, if you're bringing in lots of sales and seem happy with your situation, why should the typical broker say anything to rock the boat and cut back on the office's cut of your deals?

Therefore, expect to politely insist (demand) a bigger split when the time is right, as detailed above. After all, you now have the leverage. If you're a good producer, you should be able to go to any number of other offices and get a better commission split. You know it. And your broker should know it.

If your broker is unwilling to increase your split even after you request it, politely ask why. Maybe there is a logical reason that your particular sales haven't brought in all the wealth you thought they did. Perhaps there were complications, legal snafus, or other problems.

But, if your broker says something like he or she simply can't afford to give you more and still maintain the office, move on. Your broker should not be a charity case and you should not be a donor.

Invest in Real Estate Yourself

Would you buy from a stock broker who didn't invest in stocks? Well, then, what about buying from a real estate agent who didn't invest in property?

I'd think twice in the above circumstances, and I suspect so would anyone else with whom you deal. In fact, many agents when talking with clients will at some point purposely bring up the fact that they own their own home and some may even mention they have rentals as well. This suggests that they have confidence in the market and expect to eventually make money on their properties. In short, it puts people at ease when they feel that you're in the same investment boat as they're in.

After all, don't you believe in the very product that you're selling? If you don't, perhaps selling stocks, bonds, gold, or even fishing lures might be a better career option.

Of course, there's another compelling reason to buy property. As an agent, you will inevitably come across good deals that you can take advantage of. When that happens, either by yourself or with partners (other agents, investors, even your broker), you should make an effort to invest.

Over time, many agents put together a strong portfolio of properties that acts as the best retirement account in the world. It might take a while, 15 or 20 years would not be exceptional, but then, if you had a dozen properties paying themselves off (from rental income) and producing strong cash flow, you could slow down, even retire.

Today, millions of Americans look to real estate as the ultimate investment vehicle. They will come to you and ask you to help them make their fortunes by investing in property. Should you do any less for yourself than you do for your clients?

Always Be Honest and Aboveboard

Occasions will arise when you will be tempted to commit a minor infraction of real estate law or ethics either by commission or omission.

It happens sooner or later to everyone in the field. You may realize that simply by telling a little fib, or perhaps forgetting to mention some little defect in a home or a contract, you can get a quick sale. And you further realized that chances are that no one will ever be the wiser.

Of course, all the real estate books tell you to take the high road and do the right thing. But, when faced with the reality of the situation, it actually may be a hard choice.

When faced with this situation, I suggest you think not just of what the books say, not of the short term, but of the longer term. It's important to realize that there's a slippery slope where committing even a minor infraction makes it so much easier to commit another and even bigger one next time.

After a while, invariably someone who takes a shortcut or who overlooks the rules gets a bad reputation among other agents—and then even among buyers and sellers. And then, almost without fail, something blows up. And the real estate board and maybe even the regulators in your state get involved. And then, at best, there goes your career in real estate.

TRAP

 The real problem is that there is so much opportunity in selling real estate to omit an important fact or say something that will slant another person's thinking, all to get a deal.

For anyone who wants to have a long-term career in real estate, there's only one, difficult road to walk. That's being absolutely honest and aboveboard in all your dealings. It will give you a wonderful reputation. And ultimately, your reputation is what you're going to live—or fall—by.

18

Getting Off the Ground

The hardest thing about getting started is getting started.

That initial push-off is like a writer sitting down to a blank page, or an engineer looking at a blank computer screen—or an agent going into the office for the first day.

In Chapter 4 we talked about time management and how to usefully spend your first days in real estate. Time management is very helpful and can give you direction and a sense of motion, if not real accomplishment.

However, as I've said many times, nothing succeeds like success. Getting off the ground means getting listings, making deals and closing them, and getting that commission check. Many agents celebrate that first commission check with a bottle of champagne. Perhaps it's better to do so with the tenth commission check, because by that time you really know you're on your way.

For those who have already earned their tenth commission check and their twentieth and their hundredth, congratulations. You've taken off, you've got wings, you're soaring.

But for those who haven't gotten to that first commission check, or for those who have but haven't seen it multiply by many more, a real estate career at this time may seem problematic.

When Success Is Elusive

Regardless of how long you've been in the business, whether it be a week, six months, or even a year, at some point you may begin to feel that success is eluding you. Either there aren't any commission checks, or they aren't coming in fast enough, or they aren't big enough.

TRAP

Thomas Edison was once interviewed by a reporter as he was seeking a way to build the first sustainable incandescent light. The reporter asked how Edison felt about the fact that he had tried and failed over a thousand times to find a filament that would hold up to the electric current running through it and yet generate continuous light. Edison is reported to have said, "I haven't failed at all. I've had a thousand successes. I now know a thousand ways not to build a lightbulb!"

It's easy enough to get down on yourself. Maybe you've been farming an area for two months and you haven't gotten a single solid lead. Or it seems as though every time you take prospects out to see a house, they don't like it. Perhaps those few deals that you made fell apart in escrow.

Are you a failure as a real estate agent?

It's certainly easy to feel like one when things don't go well. I've never known a successful agent who didn't have a misstep here and there. Most started out slowly. But even those who were out of the gate with a bang, had times, occasionally lasting many months, when nothing went right. If this is happening to you, don't feel you're alone. It happens to almost everyone. It's part of getting started in the business.

TIP

There is nothing easier to explain than failure. It is, after all, what most people do most of the time. What's truly remarkable is success.

Take a Time-Out

When things aren't going well, it's time for a time-out. This is a pause that allows you to step back and take a good look at where you are and what you've done to get there. It's a time for reflection, a time to consider how you can change course to catch the wind.

Time-outs should last at least two days.

Spend the first day relaxing and doing things that make you feel good. Go fishing, or to a spa, bowling, or a ball game. Take the kids out to Chucky Cheese. (No, that's probably not a great idea for relieving stress!) Create a romantic evening with your spouse.

Break the gloom and let the sun shine through. Refresh yourself. Do something good for yourself. Do something that allows you to remember what a good person you are and how valuable you are to others as well as to yourself. Recapture your confidence. (Doing this doesn't mean it has to be an expensive day; money is rarely what's required to make us really feel really good about ourselves.)

On the second day, look inward. Think about what you're doing and concentrate on what you consider to be failures. Perhaps you haven't gotten enough leads. Or, you haven't been able to convert leads to listings. Or, your prospects slip away without making offers. Or your deals fall through. Or something else.

TIP

If you know someone, such as an experienced agent, or if you have a mentor, ask them for help. Tell them your feelings and see what they have to say. Often another mind can put things into a totally different perspective and show you some simple adjustments that can be done to correct the situation.

Make a List, Check It Twice

Next, make a list of all of those things you feel you've done badly. List them all. Don't overlook or downplay something; don't be soft on yourself. On the other hand, don't wallow in self-pity to the point where you put down more than you need to or exaggerate imagined failures.

Keep it simple. "Not enough leads." "Can't convert prospects to buyers." And so on.

Now go back through your list and see if you can figure out what actions of yours have caused the problems.

Is it that you simply haven't worked hard enough? If you've worked hard, have you worked smart? Reread the chapters on dealing with buyers, getting leads, converting leads to listings, and so on. Have you really been doing all that you could to be successful?

Typically, not converting leads to listings, not getting good offers from buyers, not making deals, or having them fall out of escrow can be traced down to a couple of bad habits that are repeated over and again. Bad things don't usually happen because you intend them to. They happen because there's either something you're forgetting to do or because there's something you're doing wrong. Try to find out what it is.

Look back at your actions. When did things first start going wrong? What did *you* do to cause it? What did *you* do to fail to correct it. Identify the problem.

Turn Those Negatives into Positives

A useful exercise is to take your list and turn the negatives into positives. For example, you're not getting many solid leads. Okay, how many ways have you learned *not* to get them? (Remember Edison in the TRAP above?) What have you learned about getting leads that *you should not, or should, do?*

- Did cold calling leave you cold? Then don't waste anymore time doing it. (See Chapter 5.)

- Did you fail to strike up conversations that led anywhere when talking with potential sellers? Then work on building rapport, and eliminate those talking traits that set you back.(See Chapter 7.)

- Did buyers with whom you worked for weeks buy through someone else? Then stop putting yourself down, and refresh your skills at promoting yourself. (See Chapter 7 again.)

- Did you have trouble getting started in the morning? Then don't just sit there drinking coffee—build a schedule and stick to it? (See Chapter 4.)

Try to analyze your actions to get to the wrong actions, or lack of actions, that are causing your problems. Once you've identified what you're doing wrong, like Edison, you've just had a success! You now know at least one way *not* to get leads or close escrows or whatever.

If what you've been doing doesn't work, what can you do differently that will work? Again, reread the relevant chapters, talk with experienced agents and a mentor, if available, and then take action. Start moving in the direction of success.

Avoid Nay-Sayers

Over the years I've found that while there are some people to whom you can turn for constructive advice and help, there are others to whom you shouldn't. These are people who love to tell you what's wrong with you, that you've failed, why you can't succeed, and that you should simply stop trying.

These people can be other agents, friends, associates, even loved ones such as relatives or spouses. Often they're well-intentioned; they're negative for reasons totally unrelated to you. For example, maybe they've never really succeeded themselves and, hence, don't want to see you do it. Or they're dependent on you and are afraid that if you continue, you won't make much money and that could affect their lifestyle. Or they have little imagination and can't see how a real estate agent can do well. Or . . . whatever.

When you're down on yourself, the last thing you want or need is to have someone else dump on you. Get away from the nay-sayers. Try to be with people who are positive.

What's important to remember is that there will always be periods of time in any profession when things don't go as well as anticipated. But we can learn from these times and do better in the future. Be optimistic. It's the best attitude to have. It's contagious. And it will ultimately lead you to new successes.

Traveling the High Road of Service

If there's one thing I've learned in many years of working at real estate, it's that chasing the dime doesn't work. Those whose goal is simply to make money usually are never satisfied, never consider themselves successful, and often don't actually make a lot of money.

On the other hand, those who look at real estate as a service profession, usually do very handsomely both in personal satisfaction with what they do and in their financial fortunes. When you see your role as serving people by helping them to get into homes where their families can grow, to sell homes so they can move up or sideways, to buy and sell other property, suddenly you've moved beyond mere monetary considerations. That's when real satisfaction with what you do can appear.

Of course, no one is saying that you should work for free. However, I have found that when people like what they do, when they consider their work an important and valuable contribution to others, they tend to succeed.

In short, understand and act as though what you are doing is providing a valuable service to others, and the money will follow. The money *will* follow.

TIP

Remember, your most important task is to serve your clients. When you do it well, they will love you for it, you'll feel good about it, your competitors will respect you, and you'll come home richer every day.

Index

About the Author

Robert Irwin is a real estate broker and one of America's leading experts in all areas of real estate. He is the author of more than forty books, including McGraw-Hill's best selling Tips and Traps series. For more real estate tips and traps, go to www.robertirwin.com.